YORK NOTES

The Glass Menagerie

Tennessee Williams

Notes by Rebecca Warren

 Longman

York Press
322 Old Brompton Road, London SW5 9JH

Pearson Education Limited
Edinburgh Gate, Harlow,
Essex CM20 2JE, United Kingdom
Associated companies, branches and representatives throughout the world

First published 2003

10 9 8 7 6 5 4 3 2 1

ISBN 0-582-77231-1

Designed by Vicki Pacey
Phototypeset by Land & Unwin (Data Sciences), Northampton
Produced by Pearson Education North Asia Limited, Hong Kong

CONTENTS

PART ONE

INTRODUCTION

HOW TO STUDY A PLAY

Studying on your own requires self-discipline and a carefully thought-out work plan in order to be effective.

- Drama is a special kind of writing (the technical term is **genre**) because it needs a performance in the theatre to arrive at a full interpretation of its meaning. Try to imagine that you are a member of the audience when reading the play. Think about how it could be presented on the stage, not just about the words on the page.

- Drama is always about conflict of some sort (which may be below the surface). Identify the conflicts in the play and you will be close to identifying the large ideas or themes which bind all the parts together.

- Make careful notes on themes, character, plot and any **subplots** of the play.

- Why do you like or dislike the characters in the play? How do your feelings towards them develop and change?

- Playwrights find non-realistic ways of allowing an audience to see into the minds and motives of their characters, for example **soliloquy**, aside or music. Consider how such dramatic devices are used in the play you are studying.

- Think of the playwright writing the play. Why were these particular arrangements of events, characters and speeches chosen?

- Cite exact sources for all quotations, whether from the text itself or from critical commentaries. Wherever possible find your own examples from the play to back up your opinions.

- Always express your ideas in your own words.

These York Notes offer an introduction to *The Glass Menagerie* and cannot substitute for close reading of the text and the study of secondary sources.

The Glass Menagerie is the ideal introduction to Tennessee Williams' work. In this play the dramatist explores themes that would preoccupy him throughout his life: human fragility, desire, deception, illusion, the awkwardness of negotiating the past while struggling to cope with the present and future. Williams also creates a cast of memorable characters, who appear in many guises in his later works. Most notable here is the characterisation of flawed but ultimately sympathetic female figures: Amanda, the unrealistic but determined mother, and her vulnerable daughter, Laura. In his first commercial success, Williams succeeds in taking us into their private world in a truly touching way.

The male characters are Williams' types too. Tom, the narrator, is a guilty dreamer, who hankers after a more fulfilling life elsewhere. The gentleman caller, Jim, is better adjusted to his circumstances, but also a fantasist. The third male character, Mr Wingfield, who never makes an appearance, casts a long shadow over the proceedings. One of the most moving qualities of this play is its generous even-handedness. Williams does not moralise in *The Glass Menagerie*; we are asked to observe and understand, but not condemn, his fragile cast.

Early commentators were sometimes puzzled by the play's lack of action. Unlike other successful dramatists of the 1930s and 1940s, Williams chose to construct his story in a loose and episodic way, paying as much attention to the staging as to the plot. The play is not split into acts, and scenes are not all of a similar length. Williams is trying to capture and portray the movements of memory, and in order to do this, he shifts the focus from one character to another and introduces a narrator who looks back on the events of a painful period of his life. Williams' use of lighting and music was particularly original and striking at the time the play was first performed, and, in order to arrive at a full understanding of *The Glass Menagerie*, the reader needs to pay close attention to Williams' dramatic technique, which is not naturalistic. Williams was interested in the theatre as a specific medium, and his conception of the **genre** was informed by his love of poetry. It is 'stage poetry' that he hoped to achieve in this drama. In order to make best use of the opportunities the stage provides, Williams incorporated expressionistic techniques such as the screen device and **tableau vivant**. The dialogue is allusive, props are symbolic, and characterisation detailed and precise. Williams is also very sure about where his audience should be focusing at any given moment. The stage directions make it plain that it is the silent Laura who is the central figure, rather than her more loquacious relatives.

Williams' use of artificial theatrical devices does not overwhelm the simple but affecting tale that Tom Wingfield tells. In fact, the use of an anguished narrator adds to the emotional appeal of the play. We are not kept in suspense about the outcome of *The Glass Menagerie*, so we have plenty of time to consider the ways in which the characters interact, and, more importantly, how they feel. Williams' use of symbolism helps the reader arrive at a deeper understanding of the cast and their motives. The glass menagerie stands out, coming to represent all the fragile dreams that consume the people on stage.

The twenty-first century reader needs to pay close attention to the historical context of *The Glass Menagerie*. While it is undoubtedly true that Williams is most interested in portraying the inner lives of a small group of people, he also expects his audience to grasp the significance of events going on in the wider world, and how they affected people. The events of the play take place in the late 1930s, during the Great Depression, one of the bleakest periods in twentieth century American history. In a more optimistic age Amanda would not have to cling so desperately to her son. Her fear that Tom will abandon the family is more easily understood if the reader is aware that up to twenty-five per cent of the workforce were unemployed during the worst years of the Depression. Tom is exceedingly lucky to have a job of any kind. If we consider how slim his chances are of finding a better life, perhaps his struggle to leave St Louis is heroic as well as foolhardy. Williams' allusions to other times and places – the Old South, the First World War, Mexico, the South Sea Islands – help him to explore the themes of conflict and dreams that interest him.

Finally, *The Glass Menagerie* makes intriguing reading for anyone interested in the complex and imaginative ways in which the dramatist transforms the material of his own life for artistic purposes. Tennessee Williams drew heavily on his memories and family experiences when he was writing this play. During the early 1940s Williams made several attempts to write about his sister Rose, whose tragic history affected him deeply. Some critics have suggested that *The Glass Menagerie* is an elegy for Rose and a plea to be released from the guilt Williams felt when he was unable to save her from the lobotomy that destroyed her personality. The playwright is also perhaps trying to come to terms with his feelings about his mother and father, whose lives provided him with the raw materials he needed to write the characters of Mr and Mrs Wingfield. In Tom Wingfield, who shares the same first name as his creator (Tennessee was a nickname), we have a portrait of the writer as a young man. The dreams that preoccupy Tom – adventure, escape, the creative life of the wanderer – are the dreams that Williams hoped he would himself fulfil.

PART TWO

SUMMARIES & COMMENTARIES

The Glass Menagerie was first performed in Chicago in December 1944. The play opened on Broadway the following year, enjoying a run of 561 performances and winning the New York Drama Critics' Circle Award, the Donaldson Award and the Sidney Howard Memorial Award. The first London production, directed by John Gielgud, opened in 1948. Subsequently there were major revivals in New York and London in 1965.

The first film version of the play, which was not a faithful adaptation of Williams' text, was made in 1950, directed by Irving Rapper. Tennessee Williams was appalled by what he considered 'the most awful travesty of the play I've ever seen ... horribly mangled'. In order to fit in with the conventional Hollywood happy ending typical of women's pictures of the time, several changes were made to the plot and characterisation. Laura was portrayed as a much more normal girl, whose reluctance to go to school is explained by the cruel treatment she receives at the hands of a teacher. At the end of the film she is content to see Tom leave because she is preparing to meet a new gentleman caller. Two popular screen versions of the play have been produced in the last thirty years. In 1973 Katharine Hepburn and Sam Waterston appeared in an ABC production, while Paul Newman directed his wife Joanne Woodward and John Malkovich in the Cineplex Odeon film of 1987.

In the United States the play was first published by Random House in 1945. For the preparation of these Notes, *A Streetcar Named Desire and Other Plays*, Penguin Twentieth-Century Classics, 1962, was used. All page references in these Notes refer to this edition. (The third play included in the collection is *Sweet Bird of Youth*.) The recent Methuen Student Edition of the play, which includes a detailed introduction by Stephen J. Bottoms, is also well worth consulting: *The Glass Menagerie*, Methuen, London, 2000.

The play opens with the narrator, Tom Wingfield, looking back on his life with his mother and sister in a run-down ground floor apartment in St Louis in the late 1930s. Tom is dressed as a merchant sailor and he stands on the fire-escape of the building his family inhabited. He begins by offering the audience a brief 'social background' (p. 235) to the story he will tell, painting a picture of an uncertain and depressing world. Then he moves on to introduce the characters who will bring to life his 'memory play' (p. 235); Amanda (his mother), Laura (his sister) and the gentleman caller who will appear in the final scenes. Tom also mentions a fifth character, his father, who abandoned the family a long time before the events he narrates. In spite of appearing only as a smiling, 'larger-than-life-size photograph' (p. 235), Mr Wingfield remains a palpable presence in his family's lives.

Tom is a poet who works as a clerk for a shoe company. He dislikes his job intensely and dreams of escape. He also feels stifled by his family, most especially his mother. Yet he knows that he is depended upon as the breadwinner. Amanda fights valiantly to hold her fragile family together, but, like Tom, she is preoccupied with her own fantasies. They take two forms; elegiac recollections of her youth in Blue Mountain as a popular young Southern belle, and musings about a gentleman caller who will marry her daughter and make the future secure. Laura, meanwhile, lives in a world of her own, playing her father's old records and polishing her glass collection. Shy and withdrawn, she is acutely self-conscious about her physical 'defect' (p. 247).

In the first scene Tennessee Williams establishes the tension that characterises life in the Wingfield household. Tom and Amanda bicker over a meal. When Tom retreats to the sidelines to smoke, Amanda regales her children with stories of her youth, describing what happened to a number of the gentlemen callers she received before her marriage. She clearly hopes that Laura will soon attract an admirer herself, but the girl knows that she is not as popular as her mother was. In the next scene it becomes clear that Laura's shyness and disability have prevented her from functioning in the world outside the apartment. Amanda discovers that her daughter has dropped out of a secretarial course in business school because of her nerves. Deeply disappointed, Amanda decides that marriage is the only answer for Laura – she will never be able to support herself financially in a career. It is to be Tom's job to locate and invite home an eligible young man.

Amanda also takes practical steps to 'feather the nest and plume the bird' (p. 248). She conducts 'a vigorous campaign on the telephone' (p. 248), roping in subscribers to a magazine called *The Home-maker's Companion* in a brave attempt to earn enough money to buy Laura new clothes. When Tom breaks the news that one of the other workers at the warehouse, Jim O'Connor, has accepted an invitation to dinner, Amanda is delighted. Laura, however, is fearful. She had a secret crush on Jim at high school and knows that seeing him again will be nerve-racking.

On the night of the dinner Laura retreats to the sofa while her mother entertains Jim with charming Southern hospitality. Amanda even manages to overcome the embarrassment of the lights going out, a result of Tom's failure to pay the light bill. Jim is sent into the living room with a candelabrum. Amanda wants him to draw Laura out. Jim's kindness and easy manners put Laura at her ease; she discusses her glass collection with him and even manages to accompany Jim in a waltz. The young man also outlines his own ambitions and, moved by his companion's delicate prettiness and lack of confidence, kisses Laura. This is the turning point in her existence. For a moment Laura comes fully to life.

Almost immediately '*the sky falls*' (p. 309). Jim reveals a secret – he is engaged to be married to a girl named Betty and will never call again. Amanda reappears with a jug of punch and the evening comes abruptly to an end. Before he leaves, Laura gives Jim the broken unicorn as a souvenir (its horn was snapped off when the couple bumped into the table it was resting on while they were dancing). After the gentleman caller's departure Amanda turns on Tom, accusing him of stupidity and selfishness; he has made fools of them all by bringing home another girl's fiancé. Tom smashes his glass on the floor and storms out to the movies.

In his final narration, delivered while Amanda silently comforts Laura, Tom informs us that he was fired from his job at the shoe company shortly after this disastrous evening. He then made his escape and began his life as a drifter, following 'in my father's footsteps' (p. 313). But this new roving life has not brought him happiness. Tom has been unable to forget his sister, and feels guilty about deserting her. Like Amanda and Laura, he remains trapped by the past.

SCENE 1   Tom Wingfield, the narrator, introduces the other
characters in the play. He clashes with his mother, Amanda,
during a meal. Amanda describes an afternoon in her
girlhood when she received seventeen gentlemen callers and
jokes with her daughter Laura about the prospect of young
men calling that afternoon

In his opening narration Tom tells us that he will 'turn back time' (p. 234)
in order to present his 'dimly lighted' and 'sentimental' 'memory play'
(p. 235). He begins with a brief description of America in the 1930s, also
offering a snapshot of events in Europe. He introduces the characters who
will appear: his mother Amanda, sister Laura and 'a gentleman caller who
appears in the final scenes' (p. 235). Tom tells us that there is another
symbolic character to take account of, too: his father 'who left us a long
time ago' (p. 235). We learn that Mr Wingfield 'gave up his job with the
telephone company' (p. 235) and was last heard of in Mexico. His photographic portrait hangs on the living room wall.

Amanda's voice can be heard through the portières. Mother and
daughter are seated at a table. Tom joins them for the meal. Amanda
complains about the way Tom eats, comparing him to an animal. This
exasperates him and he withdraws to have a cigarette. Amanda chides him
for smoking too much. Laura offers to bring in the dessert, but Amanda
tells her to remain seated so that she can 'stay fresh and pretty' for gentleman
callers (p. 237). Amanda fetches the blancmange herself, regaling her
children with a frequently told tale about her girlhood in Blue Mountain.
Tom and Laura humour her, knowing that their mother loves to relive the
afternoon when she received seventeen gentlemen callers. Amanda describes
what happened to some of her beaux. She makes a reference to her marriage,
but we do not learn why she accepted Mr Wingfield's proposal.

Talking about her past has clearly put Amanda in an optimistic
mood, for she enquires playfully about her daughter's romantic prospects.
How many callers is Laura expecting? The question makes the girl nervous
and she 'slips in a fugitive manner through the half-open portières' (p. 239), in
order to escape further teasing. But she is not let off the hook. Amanda
calls after her. Tom, who is less indulgent than his sister, groans. Laura is
forced to admit that she is not popular with men.

On the surface it seems that very little of any consequence occurs in the opening scene – *The Glass Menagerie* is clearly not going to be a plot-driven play. So how does Tennessee Williams succeed in drawing us in?

The reader must look to the staging for answers. The playwright has a clear vision of how the set should look, and the language he uses makes it plain that the Wingfield apartment in St Louis is a run-down and depressing place to live. The most important detail, to which Williams returns several times during his opening description, is the fire escape.

The dramatic significance of the fire escape becomes apparent when Tom enters dressed as a merchant sailor. He looks incongruous in this setting. Clearly, he has succeeded in moving on. So why return? When he speaks, we learn that his memories have drawn him back. They are more powerful than his urge to escape: the staircase Tom stands on represents a dream that has gone sour.

Tom's narration in Scene 1 is characterised by the quiet desperation Williams hopes to convey with the setting. The narrator is apologetic; he is 'the opposite of a stage magician' (p. 234), he can only offer 'truth in the pleasant disguise of illusion' (p. 234). The phrasing suggests that the 'truth' of *The Glass Menagerie* will be far from comforting. The 'social background' (p. 235) Tom outlines sounds harsh; the economy of America is 'dissolving' (p. 234), the middle classes stumble about blindly, there are violent 'disturbances of labour' (p. 234). In Europe things are worse: 'In Spain there was Guernica' (p. 234, see Glossary). The Thirties were clearly a challenging decade to live through. But having given us a factual account of a dismal age, Tom then insists that the play we will watch 'is not realistic' (p. 235). This statement goes to the very heart of Williams' dramatic technique: his purpose as a writer is to explore subjectivity – the inner, imaginative lives of his characters. It is thus entirely apt that Tom is a poet trapped in a tedious warehouse job. We learn little about Tom as an employee in the course of the play; what really count are his extra-curricular activities and aspirations. They are the real Tom.

A consideration of some of the other staging techniques used in this opening scene suggests that the playwright is concerned with psychological truth rather than **naturalistic** presentation. Williams' screen device and magic lantern slides are self-consciously theatrical. Some of the items that adorn the Wingfield apartment will prove to be **symbolic**; the *scores of transparent glass animals* (p. 234), the portrait of Mr Wingfield. There is a transparent fourth wall which ascends when the play begins and comes down during Tom's final speech; the gauze portières are transparent too. Their lack of solidity helps the audience to understand that it is in the land of memory, which is shifting and subjective. Tom links the music of the play very specifically to the processes of the mind: 'In memory everything seems to happen to music' (p. 235). He also draws attention to the lighting, which will be deliberately dim and sentimental, as befits a 'memory play'. Significantly, we learn that the gentleman caller is 'the most realistic character in the play, being an emissary from a world of reality' (p. 235).

Tom's narration is obviously poetic. He speaks metaphorically and declares that he has a 'weakness for symbols' (p. 235). In addition, Amanda suggests that her son has a theatrical streak, a temperament 'like a Metropolitan star!' (p. 236, see Glossary). She may be exaggerating, as she often does, but in Scene 3 we will see evidence of Tom's fondness for drama when he storms out after delivering a highly imaginative speech about living a life of vice and corruption. Amanda's longer speeches have been compared to operatic arias. When she talks of Blue Mountain she sounds like an actress returning to a favourite role: 'One Sunday afternoon in Blue Mountain...' she begins (p. 237). Amanda's words recall the language of fairy tales and 'Once upon a time...'. The *spot of light on Amanda*, the repeated screen legend, '*OÙ SONT LES NEIGES*', and image, '*AMANDA AS A GIRL ON A PORCH, GREETING CALLERS*', reinforce the impression of ritual, role playing and myth that the playwright is carefully establishing. This will be an important theme in the play.

Finally, the use of a narrator is an *undisguised convention* (p. 234). From the very start we are aware that *The Glass Menagerie* is Tom's version of family life. And he seems to have complete control of his

y

material; he cues in music and lighting, as well as choosing the moment when we will first see his family. Williams sets Tom up to frame events and comment on them. Critics have suggested that this creates a distance between audience and action. Is this distance increased because Tom is also a character and participant in the tale he tells, or does his double role enable Williams to demand greater empathy from the audience? Perhaps, in spite of the self-conscious theatricality of the play, it is impossible *not* to feel emotional identification with *all* the Wingfields (and later with Jim). This is partly because each character is allowed to take centre stage at some point in the play, and because we swiftly come to realise that silence can be as important as speech – especially in Laura's case. Let us look more closely at the characters to see where their emotional appeal lies.

The situation in which the Wingfields find themselves attracts sympathy. Tom hints that the family is lost, and perhaps confused, as they wait for 'the long-delayed but always expected something that we live for' (p. 235). The phrase suggests definite but unfocused hope. That this fervent longing is attached to an individual hints that, inevitably, the Wingfields will be disappointed. It is unrealistic to expect salvation from 'a nice, ordinary, young man' (p. 228). The family has suffered loss. Mr Wingfield's abandonment of them has led to financial hardship. It has also mentally scarred Amanda, Tom and Laura. In the first scene this is confirmed when Amanda stops short when discussing her beaux: 'And I could have been Mrs Duncan J. Fitzhugh, mind you! But – I picked your *father!*' (p. 239). Her tone has changed. While describing the men she dated prior to her marriage she has been able to maintain a certain breeziness, but now she is lost for words. The pause after 'But' confirms this. Amanda does not return to the topic of her husband again in this scene. The reality of her circumstances is too painful and she prefers to concentrate on the fantasy that Laura will be visited, as she was, by a string of eligible bachelors.

Laura's reaction to her mother's words is significant. Immediately after the reference to her father, she rises from her seat and changes the subject. This is her way of deflecting pain. As the play progresses,

we see Laura playing her father's victrola compulsively. She listens to
Mr Wingfield's records when she is on her own, or when she feels
threatened and scared. Is she seeking a comfort that is unavailable to
her elsewhere? We will come to understand that her father's rejection
of her is something from which Laura has never recovered.

At the beginning of the play Tom's attitude to his father is more
ambiguous. Tom does not speak after Amanda mentions Mr
Wingfield, so we cannot be sure what he is thinking. He 'throws
down the paper and jumps up with a groan' (p. 239) when Amanda
starts chattering about gentlemen callers; his ire is not directed at the
absent man. His restless movements fit in with his impatient
utterances earlier in the scene (p. 237). Altogether, Tom is less
forbearing than his sister about Amanda's need to glorify the past. If
we also take into account his narrator's seaman's uniform and poetic
observation that his father 'fell in love with long distances ... and
skipped the light fantastic out of town ...' (p. 235), it is possible to
argue that Tom envies his father and hopes to emulate him. The
reader also needs to consider the portrait on the wall when trying to
determine how Mr Wingfield and his desertion are to be viewed. The
playwright does not draw particular attention to it in this scene, but
the grinning photograph is surely ironic. How dare Mr Wingfield
smile after what he has done?

Mr Wingfield was clearly a disappointment as husband and father.
There are other disappointments that make us sympathise with the
family. Amanda's youthful idyll of romance, gentility and financial
security has failed to materialise. Her name, which means 'worthy of
being loved', is touchingly ironic. What has she left? An irritable son
whose manners fail to come up to scratch, and a daughter in danger
of becoming an old maid. And yet Amanda tries to make the best of
things. Talking herself into an optimistic frame of mind, she hopes to
buoy up her children as well as herself. Her fantasising makes her
simultaneously foolish and endearing in this scene.

While Williams undoubtedly focuses on the mother's frustrated
yearnings in Scene 1, he also draws attention to the plight of Laura.
At the end of the scene she is cruelly put under the microscope when

Amanda insists on continuing with the topic of gentleman callers. Amanda is insensitive here. Her absurd, light-hearted remarks about tornadoes and floods make Laura's misery more intense. When Laura delivers her last speech about becoming an old maid she is clearly close to tears. The contrast between Amanda's day of extraordinary triumph in Blue Mountain, and the sad reality of Laura's non-existent social life, is affecting. Perhaps Amanda is at fault in Scene 1? Surely she should be protecting rather than exposing her shy child?

Williams undercuts the sentimentality of the scene with **irony**. In character, Tom's responses to Amanda's arias are almost sarcastic: 'I know what's coming!', 'Again?', 'How did you entertain those gentleman callers?', 'What did he leave his widow?' (pp. 237–39). These pithy lines convey the tension in the household and show us that there are different ways of interpreting the characters. Because of Tom's authority as narrator, we will be alert to the unconscious irony of many of Amanda's utterances and actions. To begin with, there is the irony that her long opening speech about the importance of eating properly drives Tom away from the table. Here, as elsewhere in the play, Amanda achieves the opposite of what she professes she intends. It is also ironic that Amanda should make such a fuss of Laura being the 'lady this time' and staying 'fresh and pretty' (p. 237) when it is painfully obvious that the girl wants to avoid attention of any kind. Ironically, when the gentleman caller does finally appear in Scene 6, it will be Amanda's charm offensive that puts him at his ease, just as it is the mother who *flounces girlishly* (p. 239) in this scene, not the daughter. It is ironic that Amanda insists on old-fashioned Southern language ('little sister', 'I'll be the darky') and manners in a dingy, urban dwelling.

The long catalogue of beaux she received in Blue Mountain is the most impressive example of unconscious irony in Scene 1. Amanda is oblivious to the fact that her recollections are depressing rather than romantic. Many of her admirers have died in violent circumstances. And then, of course, there is the fact that Amanda chose the elusive Mr Wingfield over a number of illustrious and wealthy young men. By the time the scene ends, we know that we cannot trust Amanda's judgement.

a dissolving economy the Wall Street Crash of 29 October 1929 was the
beginning of the Great Depression, a period which meant financial ruin and
hardship for a vast number of Americans (see Historical Background)
Guernica the holy city in the Basque Country in Northern Spain. During the
Spanish Civil War Guernica was almost wiped out by the German allies of
Franco's troops in 1937
a Metropolitan star the Metropolitan Opera house in New York was the city's
most famous and prestigious opera venue
the darky a black servant; a reference that reminds us of Amanda's Southern
roots. During the eighteenth and nineteenth centuries the Southern economy
was dependent on slave labour
prominent young planters of the Mississippi Delta owners of large cotton
plantations in the South
turned up their toes to the daisies a euphemism for dying and being buried
the Midas touch Midas was the legendary king of Phrygia who turned
everything he touched to gold

SCENE 2   **Amanda discovers that Laura has dropped out of business
school. She is concerned about the future. Laura reveals her
liking for a boy she knew in high school**

Laura sits polishing her glass collection. Her mother returns home in a
dejected state. Amanda has been to the Rubicam business college to check
on Laura's progress, only to find that her daughter has not been there for
some time; in fact, she dropped out 'after only a few days' attendance'
(p. 243). This is because Laura could not cope with the strain of college.
When she was asked to complete a speed-test, Laura 'broke down
completely – was sick at the stomach and almost had to be carried into the
wash-room' (p. 243). Rather than admit her failure, Laura has spent the
past six weeks walking in the park and visiting the art museum, zoo and
movie theatres. Amanda seems as desolate as her daughter; all her 'hopes
and ambition' for Laura have 'gone up the spout' (p. 244). She is fearful
about the future, asking plaintively, 'So what are we going to do with the
rest of our lives?' (p. 245).

Rallying a little, Amanda returns to the subject of men. Laura is as
uncomfortable discussing this topic as she was in Scene 1. Twisting her
hands nervously, she reluctantly says that she liked a boy called Jim once.

y

Amanda is disappointed when she learns that he was a high school boy, and that Laura's only souvenir is the year-book. Jim was not a proper boyfriend, just an acquaintance. In school he dated 'the best-dressed girl at Soldan', Emily Meisenbach. Laura assumes that they 'must be married by now' (p. 246). Laura also reveals Jim's nickname for her, 'Blue Roses'. Amanda suddenly gets up *with a spark of revival* (p. 246) and declares that Laura will marry: she must 'develop charm – and vivacity' (p. 247). Laura is doubtful. She believes that her physical disability makes her completely undesirable.

In Scene 1 Williams focused mostly on Amanda and her past. Here we learn more about Laura's sad history. All the screen images and legends in this scene are designed to shed light on Laura's character and feelings. In particular, the repeated screen image of Blue Roses perfectly expresses the girl's strange, unique fragility. Blue is a cool colour, suggesting that Laura cannot cope with intense emotion.

When we first see her in Scene 2 Laura is content, alone in her own little world of glass. This is the only time in the whole play when she is fully at ease. The props and costume Williams describes reinforce her fragility; she is seated on a *delicate ivory chair at the small claw-foot table* (p. 241), wearing a soft violet kimono. Violets traditionally symbolise modesty, while the choice of a kimono makes Laura seem like an exotic flower. Like a tropical flower, Laura wilts when she is exposed to the harsh reality of life outside her own chosen domain, the apartment. Laura's other haunts make it plain that she prefers solitude, especially the dark movie theatre, which is also Tom's preferred bolt hole. Gradually, Williams is building up a picture of a girl whose life is suspended. Or, as Amanda says, 'I thought you were an adult; it seems that I was mistaken' (p. 242). Laura has been unable to make the transition to adulthood. Later in the play, we will learn that her favourite piece of glass is a unicorn, which she acquired when she was eleven years old. At one of the most tense moments in this scene, when Amanda reaches the end of her account of Laura's ignominious career at the business school, the girl crosses to the victrola to wind it up – clear proof, if any more were needed, that Laura wishes to remain in the past. Like her mother, she is deeply attached to her memories.

We suspect that Laura's feelings about Jim are precious to her. In what seems to be a deliberately casual manner, she says that she 'came across his picture a while ago' (p. 245). Laura is protecting herself from her mother. She knows that she is going to dash Amanda's hopes again when she has to explain that she and Jim were simply on friendly speaking terms. Was Laura content to worship her idol from afar? It seems natural to her that Jim, who was a successful student, should have dated and married a pretty girl, but her comments about Emily may also suggest that she was jealous ('She never struck me, though, as being sincere' p. 246). Nevertheless, Laura clings to her positive memories of Jim's 'wonderful voice', grin and the precious nickname 'Blue Roses'. There is a touch of **irony** here. Jim misheard the details of her illness, so her nickname is based on a mistake. In Scene 7 Jim will make another, much more devastating mistake when he kisses Laura.

Laura's relationship with her mother comes under the spotlight in this scene. Is it destructive? In Scene 1 Laura indulged Amanda when she wanted to retell stories from her youth, but it seems that the mother cannot – or will not – allow her daughter the same freedom to invent herself. She wants Laura to succeed on *her* terms. We know that Amanda is thinking of herself and not Laura at the end of the scene when she talks about charm and vivacity, for she turns to the portrait of Mr Wingfield. Or perhaps Amanda is hoping that some of her husband's charm has rubbed off on her daughter. However we choose to interpret the closing moments of the scene, we know that charm brings disappointment. Does Amanda really want her daughter to lay herself open to the suffering that an unsatisfactory relationship brings? Is marriage at any cost really the answer for Laura?

It is easy to condemn Amanda. Her use of third person pronouns in this scene ('Is that the future *we've* mapped out for ourselves?', 'What is there left but dependency all *our* lives?' p. 245; my italics), suggests that she is pinning all her hopes on her daughter. Amanda cannot resist the role of martyr, making heavy weather of Laura's failures as she rolls her eyes and leans dramatically against the door frame: uttering exaggerated reproaches: 'I wanted to find a hole in the ground and hide myself in it for ever!' (p. 242). She forces her daughter to sit through a humiliating account of her time at Rubicam, concentrating on her own feelings, but not sparing Laura's. However, her speech about dependency shows us that Amanda is not entirely selfish. She knows that the lot of the unmarried female is 'pitiful' (p. 245). Ironically, Laura would probably cope with the kind of humble existence Amanda describes. Unlike her mother and brother she does not want to escape from the apartment; it is not a prison to her.

Might we then see Amanda's determined optimism as admirable? Her refusal to accept defeat is necessary. Laura is too withdrawn to find her own way in life, so a path must be found for her. Amanda's choices for her daughter may be misguided and desperate, but her maternal concern is genuine. Amanda's last speech in Scene 2 can be seen as generous. She tries to increase Laura's self-esteem by telling her that her disability is only a 'slight disadvantage' which is 'hardly noticeable' (p. 247). Ironically, of course, it is too late for kind words. Amanda has spent most of the scene concentrating on her daughter's deficiencies, and Laura is far too familiar with the 'awful suffering look' (p. 245) that suffuses her mother's face when she is disappointed, to believe in a vision of herself as a pretty charmer. At the end of the scene, roles are reversed. Laura has bumped back down to reality, while Amanda has taken herself in with another fantasy.

DAR The Daughters of the American Revolution was a conservative and patriotic women's organisation founded in 1890. Members were descendants of those who had fought in the American War of Independence (1775–83). Amanda's membership confirms her conventional and old-fashioned outlook

Famous and Barr the largest department store in St Louis

victrola a wind-up gramophone

picture of Jesus's mother in the museum presumably a *pieta*, a representation of Mary, mourning the dead body of Christ; a pieta is a symbol of human suffering

The Pirates of Penzance a comic opera by W. S. Gilbert and Arthur Sullivan, written in 1879

SCENE 3   **Amanda is selling subscriptions to a magazine. She
continues to hope that Laura will attract a gentleman caller.
After a row with his mother, Tom refuses to apologise and
storms out to the movies, striking the shelf which houses
Laura's glass animals as he leaves**

Time has passed. It is now spring. Tom tells us that finding a gentleman
caller for Laura has become Amanda's 'obsession' (p. 248). Laura is
frightened, but her mother is utterly determined that success is possible.
Amanda has taken a job selling magazine subscriptions to *The Home-
maker's Companion* by telephone. We see her talking to a woman called Ida
Scott, who hangs up on her. When the lights go up again, Laura is cringing
as her mother and brother quarrel violently behind the portières. It is not
immediately clear what has caused the trouble, but Tom seems to resent his
mother's interference in his life. He complains that Amanda is driving him
mad, confiscating his books and not giving him space to breathe. He
resents having to make a slave of himself at Continental Shoemakers to pay
the rent. Moreover, he isn't even allowed to say that he dislikes his job.

Amanda tries furiously to make Tom listen, but he has run out of
patience. His response to her anxious accusation that he is jeopardising his
job by staying out late and turning up for work in an exhausted state, is
sarcastic and eventually cruel. Pointing at his father's picture he says, 'Why,
listen, if self is what I thought of, Mother, I'd be where he is – GONE!' (p.
252). When Amanda grabs at him, he towers over her, launching into a
tirade about leading a violent double life, which terminates when he calls
his mother an 'ugly – babbling old – *witch*' (p. 252). Tom tries to make a
hasty exit, but in his frenzy he tears his coat and hurls it across the room,
striking Laura's glass collection. Both women are deeply upset. Laura '*clings
weakly to the mantel with her face averted*' while Amanda is '*stunned and
stupefied*' (p. 253) by her son's verbal attack. Tom picks up some of the
broken glass, but is unable to speak to his sister.

The opening narrative sets the tone for the scene that will follow.
Tom is sarcastic and prickly from the start. Is he mocking his mother
when he talks about her 'calculations', 'logical steps' and 'obsession'?
We get a clear picture of his irritation when he says that 'the image of
the gentleman caller haunted our apartment' (p. 248). Tom's grim

mood hints that we are correct to suspect that Amanda is relying on him to bring home the 'spectre … hope' (p. 248) that will save the family. We know that Amanda's project is doomed when Tom says that the gentleman caller's presence 'hung like a sentence passed upon the Wingfields' (p. 248).

Amanda's dream is made to sound as absurd as it is futile. It is extremely **ironic** that a woman whose own marriage failed should be 'roping in subscribers' to 'one of those magazines for matrons' that peddle romantic stories (p. 248). Tom's description of the heroines of these preposterous tales is full of ridicule (p. 248). Amanda is further undermined by the screen images and legends that appear in the first few minutes of the scene: 'AFTER THE FIASCO –', 'YOUNG MAN AT DOOR WITH FLOWERS' and 'GLAMOUR MAGAZINE COVER'. The images are completely at odds with the reality of telephone selling. Amanda works very hard to talk up the new serial by Bessie Mae Hopper and ingratiate herself with Ida Scott, but her efforts are wasted. Ida's life is as mundane as her caller's; she suffers from a sinus condition and hangs up when she smells burning, ignoring Amanda's ecstatic references to *Gone With the Wind*. It is ironic that Amanda's campaign to sell a matron's magazine is intended to benefit a daughter who refuses to see herself as a romantic heroine.

It is significant that Tom loses his temper when Amanda encroaches on his work, when he is doing, 'what I *want* to do' (p. 251). His rage shows us how seriously Tom takes his creative endeavours: poetry is his escape, and it is intolerable that he should not be able to seek refuge in his thoughts. Like Laura, Tom prefers solitude, but it proves impossible to come by at home. Just as Laura's glass-polishing was interrupted in Scene 2, Tom has to stop writing and face an interrogation about his comings and goings. Amanda is censor as well as prison guard, taking 'That hideous book by that insane Mr Lawrence' back to the library (p. 250). Lawrence's novels are characterised by unconventional relationships between men and women, in which sex is important. Amanda's disapproval of Lawrence suggests that she represents the forces of conventional morality in this play. We received early hints of her prudery in the first scene when she told Tom off for eating like an animal and insisted that she never discussed anything 'coarse or common or vulgar' with her gentlemen callers (Scene 1, p. 238). It is clear, then, that Tom's outburst at the end of the scene is a deliberate attempt to deny his mother's values. His catalogue of vice is an ironic **parody** of Amanda's aria about Blue Mountain. It becomes increasingly wild and far-fetched: 'My enemies plan to dynamite this place. They're going to blow us all sky-high some night!' (p. 252). Immediately after delivering the insulting finale which leaves Amanda speechless, he catches his arm in the sleeve of his overcoat and is left *'pinioned by the bulky garment'* (p. 252). Nevertheless, Tom deserves sympathy. He is slowly dying of boredom and frustration in the warehouse. 'I'd rather somebody picked up a crowbar and battered out my brains – than go back mornings!' (p. 251). Like Laura, Tom finds the world outside the apartment dehumanising. It drains him and crushes his spirit.

Amanda may deserve some of the scorn her son pours on her here, but we will pity her when Tom calls her an 'ugly – babbling – old *witch*'. This remark undermines Amanda's *raison d' être*. All her life she has worked hard to cultivate and hang on to her beauty and vivacious charm, but they now appear to be illusions. In the next scene she will say pitifully, 'My devotion has made me a witch and so I make myself hateful to my children!' (Scene 4, p. 257). We will also recognise the realistic and understandable fear that Amanda experiences when Tom disappears yet again to the movies. She is concerned that her son will 'jeopardize the security' (p. 251) of the whole family if he loses his job, and then, as she reasonably points out, 'How do you think we'd manage …'. While sympathising with the thwarted Tom, the reader will also appreciate Amanda's struggle for security.

In the final moments of the scene our attention undoubtedly focuses on Laura. Williams says that *'a clear pool of light'* should remain on her throughout the quarrel (p. 249), suggesting that her silent anguish is as important as the frustration her mother and brother feel. The playwright wants us to recognise that she is the one who is really under threat if the family disintegrates, a point that is underlined when there is *'a tinkle of shattering glass'* (p. 253). This is a **symbolic** moment. Having destroyed his mother's illusions verbally,

Tom now physically wrecks his sister's carefully constructed private world. However, this is an accident and Laura does not reproach her brother. Tom's inability to speak an apology and refusal to stay and make up with his mother, suggest that the male protagonist has reached a turning point. In order to save himself, he must put himself first. In his description of Tom, Williams makes this plain: 'to escape from a trap he has to act without pity' (p. 228). At the end of this harrowing scene we feel empathy for all the characters, who are now firmly established as individuals with conflicting but deeply felt desires. As we move into Scene 4 we will feel anxious about the outcome of the fight. How much longer can Amanda's hopeless romanticism survive? Is her obsession more destructive than Tom's words and actions? Or was the outcome of this scene inevitable, regardless of what has happened here?

For a detailed discussion of a section of this scene, see Textual Analysis 1.

Gone With the Wind sensational best-seller by the writer Margaret Mitchell (1900–49); published in 1936, it received the Pulitzer Prize in 1937 and was made into a film in 1939

Scarlett O'Hara the wilful romantic heroine of *Gone With the Wind*

Mr Lawrence D. H. Lawrence was a prominent and influential English novelist, who made his name with the autobiographical *Sons and Lovers* (1913). Two controversial novels, *Women in Love* (1920) and the notorious *Lady Chatterley's Lover* (1928), established Lawrence as a writer who was unafraid of tackling sexual themes

cat-houses brothels. Tom's sordid fantasies are deliberately designed to undermine his mother's romantic tales

El Diablo the Devil

SCENE 4   **Tom returns from the movies. Laura urges him to apologise to their mother. When she goes out to fetch some butter the next morning, Amanda asks Tom to bring home a gentleman caller to meet his sister**

Tom returns to the apartment at 5 a.m. He has been drinking and is unsteady on his feet. He drops and loses his door key, but Laura is waiting

and lets him in. Like her mother, Laura is incredulous that Tom can spend
so much time at the movies. When she questions him, Tom describes the
'very long programme' he sat through (pp. 254–55). The highlight of the
evening was a stage show by Malvolio the Magician. Tom gives Laura a
rainbow-coloured scarf he received from Malvolio and marvels at the
magician's most impressive trick: 'We nailed him into a coffin and he got
out of the coffin without removing one nail' (p. 255). He flops on to the
bed and begins to take off his shoes. Laura urges him to be quiet, for fear
of waking Amanda, but Tom feels that this would be sweet revenge for her
irritating morning call of *Rise and Shine*. As he is musing about a way of
getting out of what he calls 'this 2 by 4 situation' (p. 255), his father's
grinning photograph on the wall lights up. Tom falls asleep.

An hour later Amanda is preparing breakfast. She is not speaking to
Tom, so asks Laura to tell him his coffee is ready. Laura is anxious that her
mother and brother should make up and pleads with Tom to apologise. He
remains sullen. Amanda asks Laura to fetch some butter from Garfinkel's
Delicatessen. The girl is reluctant to 'charge it' (p. 256), but is persuaded to
go. She slips and falls on the stairs of the fire-escape. When Tom comes
listlessly to breakfast, Amanda ignores him, standing *'rigidly facing the
window on the gloomy grey vault of the areaway'* (p. 257). Tom slumps down
at the table, blowing on and sipping his scalding coffee. There is a good
deal of throat-clearing and coughing, but eventually Tom rises from his
seat and apologises to Amanda, who bursts into *'childlike tears'* (p. 257). She
asks Tom to promise that he will not become a drunkard and then settles
into the familiar role of nag, urging her son to eat a decent meal before
leaving for work.

But Amanda has greater things on her mind than Tom's breakfast.
She sent Laura out deliberately, so that she could have a private conversation
with her son. A few days earlier she found the girl crying. Amanda believes
that Laura's unhappiness stems from her 'idea' that Tom is 'not happy here'
(p. 259). Tom denies that he goes out at night to get away from the
apartment, preferring to deflect his mother's direct questions with a vague
statement, 'There's so much in my heart that I can't describe to *you*'
(p. 259). He defends his compulsive movie going on the grounds that he
likes adventure. Amanda isn't satisfied, telling him that he should look for
adventure in his career. Tom retorts that it is man's instinct to be 'a lover, a
hunter, a fighter, and none of those instincts are given much play at the

warehouse!' (p. 260). Mother and son squabble briefly about what Christian adults should want, and then Amanda introduces the topic she is determined to discuss: the much longed for gentleman caller. She tells Tom that he must not leave home until 'there's somebody to take your place' (p. 261). She reminds Tom of the hopeless attempts she has made to help her daughter meet people and lead a normal life. 'What can I do about it?' Tom asks, reluctant to be drawn into his mother's schemes (p. 262). He pulls on a cap and earmuffs, perhaps hoping to block out Amanda's voice. His mother continues to harry him as he stamps to the door. However, Tom eventually agrees to ask a man at the warehouse home to dinner. Amanda returns to her magazine subscriptions. As the scene fades out she is on the telephone to Ella Cartwright.

This scene has the same air of inevitability that characterised Scene 3. There is a definite sense of ritual about the way the Wingfields row and make up, signified by the pantomime of sullen silences, sly glances and coughs that mother and son go through. How many times has this scene been played out before? Is it always Tom who has to capitulate? Other elements of the scene seem ritualistic. Laura waits patiently to let Tom in after another late night. Amanda goes through her usual breakfast routine of '*Rise and Shine*' and coffee-making. Laura's reluctance to charge things at Garfinkel's because 'they make such faces when I do that' (p. 256) is stark proof of the family's permanent lack of funds. We witness the familiar row about animal instinct versus 'superior things' (p. 260). And, of course, there is Amanda's preoccupation with the gentleman caller.

But things also move on in this scene. Amanda and Tom both seem to have reached the end of their rope. In spite of his obvious irritation, Tom speaks gently to his mother on a number of occasions, recognising her fragility. We are being prepared for the moment when he calls back 'YES!' Does Tom join in with his mother's 'plans and provisions' (p. 261) because he is exhausted, or has Amanda genuinely won him over to her way of thinking? The latter seems doubtful. Right up to the moment when he agrees to invite home a clean-living young man, Tom is resistant and evasive. For her part, Amanda makes a brief but genuine attempt to accommodate Tom's viewpoint before slipping back into '*her querulous attitude*' (p. 260).

Many comments she makes suggest that Amanda has a fairly strong grasp on reality throughout this scene. And the truth makes her desperate. Tom would need a heart of stone not to be moved by words such as these; '... but – Tom – Tom – life's not easy, it calls for – Spartan endurance! There's so many things in my heart that I cannot describe to you! I've never told you but I – *loved* your father...' (p. 259). We feel for Amanda here. Starved of affection, she has had to battle with life in order to survive. No wonder she is frightened about Laura drifting along doing nothing. She knows that being a 'home girl' (p. 261) simply isn't an option unless there is sufficient money to support the home. Amanda's line, 'Oh, I can see the handwriting on the wall as plain as I see the nose in front of my face!' (p. 261) may seem melodramatic, but it is accurate. She *will* be left 'with the bag to hold' (p. 261), and she knows it, having discovered Tom's letter from the Merchant Marines. This bombshell adds urgency to the mother's pleas, which are not motivated by self-interest: '... you've got to look out for your sister. I don't say for me because I'm old and don't matter! I say your sister because she's young and dependent' (p. 261). We will not condemn the self-pity that creeps into this speech; Amanda's motherly concern is greater.

Is Tom a coward? If he is, it is because bewilderment prevents him from thinking of alternatives to Amanda's schemes. Tom suffers from the same problem that afflicts the other Wingfields: he simply does not know where to turn or what to do because he finds it difficult to face reality. His admiration for Malvolio is predictable and telling. Tom is all too aware of the **irony** of the coffin trick, as his sardonic comment to Laura shows: 'You know it don't take much intelligence to get yourself into a nailed-up coffin ... But who in hell ever got himself out of one without removing one nail?' (p. 255). Here Tom seems disgusted with himself. He accepts responsibility for his own fate, but has no answer to the question he poses. The reader will understand the implication of the question; Tom knows that ripping himself away from the bosom of his family, and most particularly his sister, is going to be a hard act to accomplish – for emotional as well as financial reasons. The religious allusions included in the description of Malvolio's show suggest that Tom is as much in need of a saviour as Amanda and Laura. He may choose to believe that man is instinctually a lover, hunter and fighter, but Tom is actually ambivalent about real-life adventure. His choice of the Merchant Marines suggests that he needs the security of an institution to give him the courage to move on.

Laura is not present for most of Scene 4, but, as in Scene 3, she is the focus. 'The Glass Menagerie' music and screen legends, 'LAURA' and 'PLANS AND PROVISIONS' demonstrate this. The girl's innocence and kindness are stressed. Laura works hard to restore harmony in the household, submitting herself to the ordeal at Garfinkel's because she wishes to avoid another row. She is a rather pathetic figure as she puts on one of her mother's old coats to go out. We are told that this garment is *'inaccurately made-over, the sleeves too short'* (p. 256). The stage directions hint that Laura cannot fulfil her mother's dreams for her. She just does not fit. Her fall on the fire-escape is **symbolic**. The world outside is treacherous and Laura is in danger when she steps out of her haven. Amanda's reference to finding the girl in tears suggests that Laura is as worried as her mother by the idea of Tom leaving. By the end of the scene the reader does not feel confident that Laura has a future of any kind to look forward to, regardless of Amanda's and Tom's machinations. Not only has she failed at business school; she was unable to utter a word to anyone at a church social function of the Young People's League.

The final moments of the scene are perhaps depressing. Amanda's stark account of her daughter's crippling shyness is followed by a second telephone call. Buoyed up by her son's acquiescence, the mother has reverted to fantasy. Significantly, Tennessee Williams withholds the outcome of the conversation; we do not know whether Ella Cartwright renews her subscription. The playwright once again undermines the leading lady's optimism. Like the other rituals in this scene, the telephone campaign is tinged with sadness.

a Garbo picture Greta Garbo (1905–1990) was a beautiful, Swedish-born star of American cinema. She was often cast as a melancholy, exotic heroine who sacrificed herself for an unattainable love

Milk Fund during the Depression, funds were collected at public events and gatherings to pay for free milk for children and the unemployed

Malvolio Malvolio is the puritanical, pompous and humourless servant in Shakespeare's comedy *Twelfth Night* (1602), who foolishly believes his mistress Olivia is in love with him. *Twelfth Night* is concerned with the gap between appearance and reality. Is Williams' choice of name for the magician ironic as well as apt?

Daumier print Honoré Daumier (1808–79) was a French realist illustrator and painter, best known for poking fun at the social customs of his day in satirical cartoons. In the late 1840s Daumier's interests shifted to painting, and producing romantic and sympathetic portrayals of working-class life. Daumier was considered to be one of the few Romantic artists who did not shrink from reality

music under: 'Ave Maria' a religious melody; the 'Ave Maria' is the 'Hail Mary'

Purina a brand of breakfast cereal

right-hand bower the jack of trumps in a card game. Amanda is implying that her son is her mainstay in life, the most important 'card' in her hand

Spartan endurance Sparta was an ancient Greek city. The population supposedly led lives of military self-discipline and frugality

Jolly Roger the flag flown by pirates with a black background and white skull and crossbones

Young People's League a group which organises activities for the young. Laura's failure here contrasts with her mother's successful membership of the DAR

horsy set on Long Island Long Island is just outside New York City. The wealthy community supposedly lead glamorous, leisurely lives

SCENE 5   Tom informs his mother that he has invited a co-worker, Jim O'Connor, to dinner the following evening. Amanda is rather put out that she has not been given more notice of the visit, but cheerfully begins her preparations

It is a short time later, still spring. The Wingfields finish their supper as dusk falls. Tom slouches on the sofa reading the evening newspaper while mother and daughter remove the dishes from the table. Amanda chides Tom for his untidy appearance. Irritated, Tom throws down the paper and crosses to the fire-escape, intending to go out for a smoke. Amanda cannot resist further chastisement, remarking that the money spent on cigarettes would be sufficient to pay for a night-school course in accounting. When she adds brightly, 'Just think what a wonderful thing that would be for you, Son!' (p. 265), Tom replies stubbornly, 'I'd rather smoke' (p. 264). He lets the screen door slam shut as he goes out, annoying Amanda. She looks up at her husband's picture, clearly concerned that her son is becoming as feckless as Mr Wingfield.

Music can be heard emanating from the Paradise Dance Hall across the alley. In his role as narrator, Tom describes the sounds and sights of the venue. He draws parallels between himself and the couples who 'could be seen kissing behind ash-pits and telegraph poles' (p. 265). Like him, they seek respite from their unadventurous and unchanging lives. Alluding to important political events in Europe, he tells us that 'All the world was waiting for bombardments!' that spring (p. 265).

Amanda follows Tom out on to the fire-escape and settles down with the newspaper. Inquisitive, she asks her son what he is looking at. A new moon shines in the sky. Tom refuses to tell Amanda what he wished for on the moon, but playfully tells her that he can guess what his mother wants. Amanda says that she wished for 'Success and happiness for my precious children!' (p. 266). Tom brings up the subject of the gentleman caller. Amanda seems taken aback to learn that an invitation has been issued. Tom toys with his mother, forcing her to grill him for further details about the prospective visitor. Amanda is alarmed when she hears that the young man will be arriving tomorrow; this gives her very little time to get things 'nice, not sloppy!' (p. 267). When Tom tells her not to make so much fuss, Amanda reminds him of the enormity of the occasion: 'Do you realise he's the first young man we've introduced to your sister?' (p. 267). Tom threatens to call the visit off unless she calms down.

Amanda drags Tom indoors for an in-depth discussion about their visitor. We learn that Jim O'Connor is of Irish descent and works as a shipping clerk, earning $85 a month. This is $20 more than Tom, but not quite enough to satisfy Amanda, who is looking ahead to Jim becoming a 'family man' on his less than 'princely' wage (p. 269). The mother ignores Tom's satirical attempts to bring her back down to earth: 'Lots of fellows meet girls whom they don't marry!' (p. 269). There is a brief interlude in which Mr Wingfield's treacherous, youthful charms are discussed, and then Jim's appearance and character are dissected. Jim is 'medium homely' (p. 270) with freckles. Amanda is pleased when she learns that he 'really goes in for self-improvement ... Radio engineering and public speaking!' (p. 270).

In her eagerness, the mother has forgotten about Laura. Tom tries to open Amanda's eyes to the truth about how outsiders view his crippled sister: '… she's terribly shy and lives in a world of her own and those things make her seem a little peculiar to people …' (p. 271). Amanda stoutly defends her daughter; if she is different from other girls, the difference is 'all to her advantage' (p. 271). Depressed by this close consideration of Laura's idiosyncrasies, Tom decides it is time to go to the movies. As usual, this upsets Amanda, but she swiftly regains her high spirits, calling her daughter out to make a wish on the moon. The dreamy girl is *faintly puzzled* (p. 272) and has to be prompted. Amanda has tears in her eyes as she tells Laura to wish for 'Happiness! Good fortune!' (p. 272).

Scene 5 is essentially a prelude to Jim's visit. Given the extreme importance Amanda attaches to this event, and the impact it will have on Laura, it is entirely appropriate that Williams devotes time to giving us some background information about the gentleman caller. How are we prepared for his entrance? Tom tantalises his mother – and the reader – when he playfully withholds information early in the scene. We know that his announcement will be a moment of great drama because the screen legend that appears when the lights come up says 'ANNUNCIATION'. Amanda responds as we would expect. She is entirely comfortable with the ritual of preparation, despite her protestations to the contrary. We know that the apartment will be successfully transformed in twenty-four hours, and that Amanda will be a great success in the role of hostess. There is a good deal of **irony** here. The mother's exuberant planning is punctuated by allusions and direct references to her absent husband. Amanda describes the social niceties of courtship in Blue Mountain. In particular, we learn how 'discreet inquiries' were made to the local minister to ascertain whether a young man drank (p. 270). Tom irreverently enquires how his mother came to make the 'tragic mistake' of uniting herself with Mr Wingfield (p. 270); it appears that the hard-drinking beau's 'innocent look' had everyone fooled. This tale of deception completely undermines Amanda's dreams of romance for Laura.

Significantly, Amanda does not dwell on her daughter's likely reaction to the news that a young man is coming to dinner. When discussing Jim's character she talks as if *she* were the potential bride.

It is easy to laugh at Amanda here; a moment earlier she was using the girlish Southern phraseology of her youth ('right-down homely', p. 270), now she talks in a pompous, matronly way. The reader will also be alert to the irony of Amanda's false claim that Jim is coming to call on her daughter. Immediately after this speech Tom informs his mother that the young man isn't even aware that Laura exists.

The rest of the scene is marked by the poignant comedy that characterises Williams' portrayal of Amanda at this point in the play. At every opportunity, the dramatist undermines his characters' yearnings for romance and escape. The screen legends are all ironic, while the music, initially cheerful ('ALL THE WORLD IS WAITING FOR THE SUNRISE!' p. 265, and 'THE ANNUNCIATION IS CELEBRATED WITH MUSIC' p. 266), becomes ominous ('THE DANCE-HALL MUSIC CHANGES TO A TANGO', p. 271). The description of the ironically named Paradise Dance Hall is striking. Initially the hall sounds charming, with its open doors, rainbow lighting and orchestra. However, it is simply another place of refuge for people who need 'compensation' for the stultifying lives they lead (p. 265). And some of the young people, momentarily deceived by 'hot swing music and liquor', will soon be participating in a war, as Tom's poetic allusion to 'the fold of Chamberlain's umbrella' makes plain (p. 265).

Amanda's children are quietly, and in Laura's case, unconsciously, subversive. Although he continues to refrain from rowing with his mother, Tom won't comb his hair or give up smoking to pay for night-school. His exit at the end of the scene represents a different kind of denial. Now he seeks refuge not from his mother, but from his wounded sister. Tom leaves after a largely tactful but truthful delineation of Laura's character. His halting speeches are little elegies of pain. Tom knows that his sister will not cope with the role of 'pretty trap' (p. 275) that is lined up for her and he wishes to avoid thinking too deeply about her prospects. His concern for his sister comes across strongly: 'She's ours and we love her. We don't even notice she's crippled any more.' (p. 271). The fierce possessiveness of the pronouns makes Tom's words touching. The lengthy discussion about Laura is ultimately depressing, in spite of the affection that is displayed. It comes after the portrait of the promising and well-adjusted Jim. The contrast between the two young people is so stark that we can only fear for the girl. When she finally comes to her mother's side, Laura is evidently more fragile than in previous scenes. As her mother's plans and provisions gather pace, she has withdrawn further into her own world. We are told that she appears *'as if called out of sleep'* and has to be seized by the shoulders and turned round so that she can see the moon (p. 272). The girl bears a startling resemblance to the 'little glass ornaments' (p. 272) she treasures so much: spontaneous movement is impossible for her now.

Tom's tone when discussing Jim frequently seems satirical. Since he cares so little about his own worldly advancement, we can be sure that he is not impressed by 'Mr O'Connor's' mania for self-improvement. In fact, Tom knows very little about Jim's character. His lack of personal interest in Jim is a hint that the young man is not the heroic lover Amanda would have him be. We might even suspect that Jim shares some of the frailties that afflict the Wingfields. Surely a freckled clerk who goes in for public speaking and radio engineering is as much of a dreamer as Tom? By the end of Scene 5 we will be eager to set eyes on the gentleman caller, but we will not be expecting anyone too extraordinary. Given the tearful closing moments of the scene, it is even possible that we will be dreading Jim's arrival – for Laura's sake.

Franco triumphs a reference to the progress of Francisco Franco's troops in the Spanish Civil War (1936–39). Franco led the Nationalists against the Republicans and was made Head of State in 1936
Washington U Washington University in St Louis, Missouri
Berchtesgaden Adolf Hitler had a villa built in this old town in Bavaria, Germany. He conducted his political affairs from here
Chamberlain's umbrella Neville Chamberlain was British Prime Minister at the outbreak of the Second World War in 1939. He believed that he had secured peace when he signed the Munich Pact in 1938, which accepted Hitler's claims on territory in Europe, but he was mistaken. When he appeared in public, Chamberlain was often seen carrying an umbrella, which became a trademark for him
James D. O'Connor Jim's Catholic background is signified by his two surnames. Catholics traditionally abstained from eating meat on Fridays, preferring fish, a

form of fasting which recalled Christ's. This is why Amanda, always concerned
to adhere to convention, says that she will serve fish
Durkee's dressing a popular brand of ready-made sauce

SCENE 6   **Jim visits the Wingfield apartment and is charmed by
Amanda. Laura is overcome by nerves and retires to the sofa
in the living room while the others eat**

In his role as narrator, Tom tells us more about Jim O'Connor, whom he
knew slightly in high school. Jim was a great success as an adolescent. In
spite of his vitality and early promise, Jim's 'speed' definitely 'slowed' after
high school; now he is holding down a job that isn't much better than
Tom's. Tom believes that Jim values him as someone 'who could remember
his former glory' (p. 272). At the warehouse Jim treats Tom with 'a
humorous attitude', calling him 'Shakespeare' because he spends time in
the toilet writing poetry when business is slack. Laura knew Jim at high
school, although Tom is not sure whether Jim remembers her. He has said
nothing about his family prior to the visit.

Before Jim and Tom return from work, Amanda and Laura have
been busy preparing themselves, and the apartment, which is adorned with
new furnishings. Amanda adjusts the hem of Laura's new dress. The girl is
nervous because of the fuss her mother is making. She becomes increasingly
uncomfortable when Amanda stuffs two powder puffs wrapped in hand-
kerchiefs down the front of her dress. Laura does not want to be turned into
a 'pretty trap' (p. 275). She looks doubtfully at herself in the mirror while her
mother goes to change.

Amanda is in a very positive frame of mind. She emerges from
behind the portières in a '*girlish frock of yellowed voile with a blue silk sash*',
carrying a bunch of jonquils (p. 276). She wore these clothes when she
received gentlemen callers in Blue Mountain. Amanda recalls the events of
the spring when she met Mr Wingfield. She switches on the rose-coloured
lamp, places the flowers in a bowl on the table and turns to Laura, who has
not yet been informed of the visitor's name. The girl is extremely disturbed
when she learns that his name is Jim O'Connor, telling her mother that she
will not be able to come to the table for dinner. Amanda refuses to humour
this 'nonsense' (p. 278). In fact, Amanda has decided that it must be Laura
who answers the door when Tom and Jim arrive. Laura panics and begs her

Y

mother to go to the door. Amanda disappears into the kitchenette to see to the food, while Laura sits on the edge of the sofa, *'knotting her fingers together'* (p. 278) and moaning softly.

When the doorbell rings, Laura again tries to persuade her furious mother to let the young men in. But Amanda will not be contradicted. The girl is forced to go to the door. She manages to escape into the front room almost immediately after she is introduced to Jim. Tom excuses his sister's shyness and hands Jim the sports section of the newspaper. Jim talks about the public speaking course that he has been taking. He warns Tom that he will be out of a job unless his attitude improves. Tom's replies are facetious and a little enigmatic; he says he is planning to change and move on, but reveals very little else. We do learn, however, that he has misappropriated the money to pay the light bill in order to join the Union of Merchant Seamen. Amanda enters through the portières. Tom is shocked by his mother's girlish appearance, but the vivacious woman quickly charms Jim.

Amanda also intends that Laura should impress the gentleman caller. Before launching into another sentimental speech about her girlhood in the South, Amanda claims that her daughter is 'in full charge of supper!' (p. 285). The food is on the table. Laura is called in. She is close to fainting. Outside, a summer storm is coming on abruptly. When Amanda sees her daughter's trembling lips and wide, staring eyes, she admits defeat. Laura is sent to rest on the sofa. Tom is asked to say grace. In the living room, Laura fights to *'hold back a shuddering sob'* (p. 287).

This is a scene of contrasts – of character, and between expectation and reality. After Tom's opening narration, which provides a link with the previous scene, it divides into three sections: Amanda's and Laura's preparations for the visit, Jim's arrival with Tom, and finally, Amanda's charm offensive. The satirical tone Tom adopts as narrator is similar to the one he used at the beginning of Scene 3. This alerts us to the fact that the social event we are to witness here will be as much of a 'fiasco' (p. 248) as Amanda's attempt to launch Laura's career at business school. Tom is again poking fun. The narrator's target is now Jim rather than his mother, but his habitual ironical detachment reminds us that Tom believes he is different. Not for him the conventional, conformist route that Jim has chosen.

Y

Jim's high school and employment histories suggest a young man who is extremely good at fitting in, unlike Tom. Jim shone in an impressive range of activities – from sport to singing – but in spite of these talents, he has had to take a dull job. Like Tom, the reader will be aware that it is **ironic** that a boy who once seemed destined for the White House should end up in a warehouse. Again, in contrast to Tom, Jim is as popular at the shoe company as he was at high school. Later in Scene 6 we come to realise that Jim is a loyal and trustworthy employee because the foreman Mr Mendoza speaks his mind freely to him. However, when he warns Tom that he is 'going to be out of a job if you don't wake up' (p. 282), Jim demonstrates that he is part of the system that Tom finds so dehumanising. This will make us critical of Jim. It is difficult to decide how to interpret Jim's influence on Tom's co-workers. Tom tells us that 'his attitude affected the others, their hostility wore off and they also began to smile at me as people smile at an oddly fashioned dog who trots across their path at some distance' (pp. 273–74). Are we glad that Tom is tolerated and has at least one co-worker with whom he is 'on friendly terms' (p. 273)? Or will we feel dismissive of his patronising friend, whose nickname for Tom is anything but original? At times, Tom's narration makes Jim sound absurd: 'He was always running or bounding, never just walking. He seemed always at the point of defeating the law of gravity' (p. 273).

Having established the differences between his two young men in the narrative section of Scene 6, Williams alerts the reader to their similarities. Almost the first topic of conversation Jim introduces when he steps on to the stage is his aspiration to get out of the warehouse; 'You know, Shakespeare – I'm going to sell you a bill of goods!' (p. 281), he says, by way of introduction to the public speaking course he is taking in order to prepare himself for 'executive positions!' (p. 281). His speech style may be more colloquial and clichéd than Tom's, but Jim's sentiments are familiar to us. Here we have another dreamer, who craves the freedom to define himself. Jim draws an interesting parallel between Tom and himself when he claims that they are both superior to the other workers at the warehouse because of their 'social poise' and ability to 'square up to people' (p. 281). Tom ignores this comment, but the reader may choose to consider it for a moment. Is Jim correct? If he is, then Tom has inherited at least some of his father's charm, which will help him make his way in the nomadic life he is ready to embark on. If Jim is merely airing his own – false and superficial – opinions and values, we might read these words as ironic. The conversation between Tom and Jim reveals another similarity between the two. Like Tom, Jim does not perhaps possess as much self-confidence as he desires. We should not be surprised by this hint of vulnerability. In the opening narration Tom told us that his presence was 'valuable' (p. 273) at the warehouse because he could remember his friend's 'former glory', clear proof that Jim needs validation from others.

It is possible to argue that both Jim and Tom face the future with a certain amount of trepidation. Both are driven by fantasies and both need their distractions (the movies and public-speaking). In this scene Williams uses the young men's dialogue as a way of revealing more information about Tom's motivation and aspirations. Williams has gentle fun with both characters, whose posturing is amusing. Tom's comments about leaving home (see pp. 282–83) can seem as boastful and hollow as some of Jim's more self-important remarks. Showing off his union card he says proudly, 'Look ... I'm a member ...I paid my dues this month instead of the light bill' (p. 283). Surely this is selfishness rather than an heroic step towards independence? Tom also proves that he enjoys the sound of his own voice, as Jim will when he lectures Laura in the next scene, 'Yes, movies! Look at them ... All of those glamorous people ... People go to the movies instead of moving!' (p. 282). Tom's style may be more original, but he is as ridiculous as Jim is when he takes himself too seriously. Ironically, it is Jim who points this out: 'You're just talking, you drip' (p. 283). For all the humour at Tom's expense, the reader will be feeling anxious by the time Amanda breaks up the conversation; the unpaid light bill is a bad omen for the women of the family. Soon they will be left to struggle along in the dark themselves. The idle talk of the young men is not as innocent or jovial as it may appear.

The same could be said of Amanda's talk. The garrulous mother works terrifically hard throughout this scene, dominating the second and final sections with her insistent talk. The repeated harrying of Laura demonstrates how destructive words have become in this play. Amanda tries various tactics to get her daughter to conform to her ideas, beginning with impatient questions – 'Why are you trembling?' (p. 274) – and commands – 'No, wait! Wait just a moment – I have an idea!' (p. 275). This bullying rattles Laura. Amanda's insistence that Laura should wear 'Gay Deceivers' stuffed in her bosom is more damaging. The statement, ' ... to be painfully honest, your chest is flat' (p. 275) suggests that Laura is faulty and must try to cover up her physical shortcomings. Given Laura's extreme sensitivity about her crippled leg and lack of popularity, this kind of criticism seems cruel, especially from her mother, who has previously insisted that her daughter's defects are barely noticeable. We quickly realise that Amanda is not thinking about her daughter's feelings – only about her appearance – and we condemn her. Even praise comes in the form of a warning: 'Now look at yourself, young lady. This is the prettiest you will ever be!' (p. 275). It is as if Laura has one chance left in life to prove that she is a worthy human being, and this is it. We have sympathy for her as she stands solemnly regarding herself in the mirror.

There are other, familiar, reasons for feeling alienated by Amanda. As usual, she spends as much time thinking about her own past as she does contemplating her daughter's future (pp. 275–77). Amanda's intention to make a 'spectacular appearance!' (p. 276) is typically vain. Is she deliberately trying to overshadow Laura, or is Amanda simply incapable of giving up the limelight? How will the reader respond when the mother steps out in her 'resurrected' frock (p. 276)? We may feel '*shocked*', as Tom is when he sees his mother (p. 284). Or perhaps we will not be surprised, since we know that Amanda lives in the past a lot of the time. It is both sad and slightly sinister that Amanda seems to have been waiting twenty years to relive her first meeting with Mr Wingfield. However, any pity or indulgence we might feel will fail to outlast Amanda's next onslaught on Laura (pp. 277–79). The mother becomes increasingly uncompromising and harsh. Laura's feelings are dismissed as 'silliness' (p. 278) and she is told 'You will come to the table. You will not be excused' (p. 278). It is hypocritical of Amanda to abandon her daughter with these words: 'Fuss, fuss – silliness! over a gentleman caller!' (p. 278). This remark belittles the miserable girl, who would have needed superhuman strength not to have been thrown into a frenzy by her mother's 'plans and provisions'. By denying that she has been making a fuss herself, Amanda also further isolates her daughter, whose desperate pleas for help have been callously dismissed.

The tension that has been building up reaches a climax when the doorbell rings. Ironically, Laura copes quite well with the ritual of being introduced to Jim. She responds appropriately to the caller's comments, even managing a polite excuse before scampering off into the front room. But this ordeal has taken its toll. In an act of kindness, Tom tries to cover for his sister when supper is ready: 'Laura is not feeling well and she says that she thinks she'd better not come to the table' (p. 285). This intentionally bland statement gives the fragile girl back some of the dignity her mother's scolding has stripped away. Tension rises again as Amanda battles with her daughter. She uses the same hectoring tone that she adopted earlier in the scene when the women were alone. This time, however, we may detect desperation in the shrill, repetitive and disjointed exclamations. In the end, ironically, the fragile daughter's terror defeats Amanda, who is not smoothing things over or offering excuses when she says *'despairingly'*, 'Why, Laura, you are sick, darling!' (p. 286).

Even now, with the **symbolic** storm coming on abruptly outside, Amanda does not give up. In the final moments of the scene she is calm enough to return to the ritual of dinner, asking Tom to say grace. The reader will be alert to the irony of this brief religious ceremony. Amanda prayed with all her heart for the gentleman caller – and his appearance has precipitated the disintegration of her daughter. Amanda's courage in the final part of the scene is both heroic and heartbreaking – very much what we would expect, given her extraordinary 'turn' as Southern belle on pp. 284–85. Her two long monologues or arias show just how tenacious Amanda is. In spite of her son's embarrassment and daughter's absence, she succeeds in charming Jim. Amanda is reliving her youth. We know this because she reverts to the language and intonation of the South, calling

Laura 'Sister', and dropping the ends off words: 'Light clothes an' light food are what warm weather calls fo' …'; 'I ran to the trunk an' pulled out this light dress – Terribly old! Historical almost! But feels so good – so good an' cool, y' know …' (p. 284). Ironically, given the high estimation she has of her powers of conversation, Amanda's chatter is inconsequential. It would be tempting to laugh, but the final lines of the second aria are distressing. Yet again Amanda returns to the topic of her faithless husband, almost as if she cannot help scratching a wound that will not heal. Here she tries to make light of her marital 'tribulations' (p. 285), but the reader knows that her love for the long distance telephone salesman has been a source of misery to her – every bit as painful as this dinner has been for Laura.

For a detailed discussion of a section of this scene see Textual Analysis 2.

White House the official residence of the President of the United States, in Washington DC

cakewalk a typical American entertainment of this period; a cake was the prize won by the person whose steps and walk were considered most pleasing and accomplished

Dardanella a popular tune of the 1920s

Ole Dizzy Dean a famous American baseball player

Gable Clark Gable (1901–60) was a famous male movie lead, nicknamed 'The King of Hollywood'. He starred as Rhett Butler in *Gone With the Wind*

angel-food cake a light sponge cake. Tennessee Williams' mother Edwina was renowned for only being able to make angel-food cake; having been used to servants, cooking was not her forte

SCENE 7 Jim is sent to keep Laura company. They discuss the glass menagerie and dance. When they bump into the table, Laura's favourite piece, the unicorn, is damaged. Jim kisses the girl, but realises immediately he has overstepped the mark. He tells her that he cannot call again because he is engaged to be married. When she finds out that Jim has a fiancée, Amanda accuses Tom of being a selfish dreamer who

has made fools of them all. Tom goes out to the movies,
while Amanda silently comforts her stricken daughter

It is half an hour later. Laura is lying on the sofa. It is still raining. Amanda, Tom and Jim are just finishing dinner when the lights go out. Amanda guesses that Tom neglected to pay the light bill. Jim jokes that he 'probably wrote a poem' on the bill (p. 289). Amanda tells her son he can help with the washing up as 'penalty' for his carelessness (p. 290), while Jim keeps Laura company 'in the parlour' (p. 290). The guest is sent into the other room with a candelabrum.

Initially, Laura is as breathless and scared as she was in Scene 6, but Jim's *'warmth overcomes her paralysing shyness'* (p. 291). The young man is unaware of the significance of the meeting for Laura. He has no idea that she has worshipped him from afar since high school. Jim tries to put Laura at ease by enquiring after her health. He sits down on the floor and makes general conversation about safe topics. Gradually, his talk becomes more personal. He flatters Laura, commenting that 'an old-fashioned type of girl' is 'a pretty good type to be' (p. 292). Embarrassed, Laura changes the subject, asking Jim whether he still sings. She finds the courage to talk about high school and the pair reminisce about their time there. Jim makes several attempts to boost Laura's confidence, telling her that she should not be so self-conscious about her leg. He mentions his own disappointments to prove to her that 'practically everybody has got some problems' (p. 295).

Like Amanda, Jim is happy reliving his glorious youth. He is delighted when Laura brings out her copy of the yearbook, *The Torch!*, which includes a picture of him in *The Pirates of Penzance*. After reflecting, *'with relish'*, that he was 'beleaguered by females in those days' (p. 296), Jim offers to 'autograph' Laura's programme for the operetta. A little later Laura asks him whether he is still 'going with' Emily Meisenbach (p. 297). When she learns that he isn't, the girl experiences a *'tumult'* of emotion, which she tries to hide by fingering one of the animals in her glass collection.

Jim asks Laura what she has been doing since high school. Laura says that she spends a good deal of time looking after her glass collection. When she turns away shyly, Jim tells the girl that he understands her 'inferiority complex' because he suffered from one, too. Believing that 'everybody excels in some one thing' (p. 299), Jim urges Laura to think of herself as superior in some way. He explains his interest in electrodynamics and radio engineering, and his intention of obtaining a job in television. Prompted by Jim, Laura talks about her hobby in more detail. She holds out her favourite piece, a unicorn, which Jim takes.

After he has replaced the unicorn on the table, Jim opens the fire-escape door. Music drifts across the alley from the Paradise Dance Hall. Jim asks Laura to dance. Convinced that she cannot, the girl is reluctant to move. But Jim is enthusiastic and swings Laura into motion. They bump into the table. The unicorn falls off and breaks. Jim is apologetic. Laura tries to ease the situation by saying that it isn't a 'tragedy' (p. 303). Relieved, Jim compliments Laura on her sense of humour and prettiness. He is genuinely touched by her gentle personality. He catches hold of her hand and kisses her. When she is released, Laura sinks on to the sofa with 'a bright, dazed look' (p. 305). Almost immediately, Jim realises that he should have restrained himself. He tries to mask his embarrassment by lighting a cigarette and offering Laura a mint.

Laura waits for Jim to speak, but when she hears what he has to say, she is devastated. Recognising that he has been brought to the apartment specifically to meet Laura, Jim explains that he cannot call again because he is in love and 'going steady' (p. 306). He is not deliberately unkind, and finds it awkward to tell the truth. In spite of her desolation, Laura smiles bravely. She carefully places the broken unicorn in Jim's hand. She is not able to speak, but Jim understands that she wants him to keep it as a 'souvenir' (p. 307). Laura moves to the victrola and winds it up.

Amanda rushes back in, carrying a pitcher of fruit punch and a plate of macaroons. She is in excellent spirits and enjoys jesting with Jim. But he is uneasy now and says he has to be going. When asked directly if he works at night, he says that he sees his girlfriend Betty in the evenings: they are to be married in June. As Jim leaves, he tells Laura he will treasure the souvenir he has been given. Magnanimously, Amanda wishes him 'luck – and happiness – and success!' (p. 310). But when the door closes behind the caller, she is wearing a puzzled expression. She does not dare to look at Laura, who is just as afraid of facing her. Amanda calls Tom in and interrogates him. She is annoyed, thinking it 'peculiar' (p. 311) that Tom should be unaware of Jim's engagement. She accuses her son of selfishly living in a dream. These familiar complaints drive Tom out to the movies. He smashes his glass on the floor and slams the door behind him. Laura screams.

The play closes with a silent pantomime. Amanda comforts Laura, who is huddled on the sofa. At the end of the speech the mother makes, the girl lifts up her head and smiles. Amanda glances at the photograph of Mr Wingfield and withdraws through the portières, while Laura blows out the candles at the end of Tom's final monologue as narrator. In this speech, Tom tells us that he was fired shortly after the evening of Jim's visit. He left St Louis and 'travelled around a great deal' (p. 313). But he has been unable to forget his sister and has been 'more faithful' to her than he intended (p. 313).

Two brief but significant sections, which serve as **prologue** and **epilogue** to the main business of the scene, frame the encounter between Laura and Jim. In the first section, the failure of the lights is symbolic. Tom's deliberate non-payment of the bill signals the beginning of a new, difficult era for Amanda and Laura, who will have to learn to live without a male breadwinner. When the lights go out, we know that those hard times have begun. The failure of the lights also signifies the hopelessness of Amanda's dreams for her daughter. It is thus poignant that the mother should react so cheerfully, attempting to turn the situation to her advantage by sending Jim in to keep Laura company in the dark. Ironically, Jim carries a candle, the light of which can be seen as a **symbol** of romance, as well as religion. At this point the Wingfields are 'in the dark' about their guest. They do not know that their supposed saviour is engaged to be married. If Amanda was aware of the truth, she would certainly think twice about exposing her fragile daughter to Jim's easy charm. The religious associations of the candelabrum are ominous. We learn that it 'used to be used at the church of the Heavenly Rest. It was melted a little out of shape when the church burnt down. Lightning struck it one spring' (p. 290). Is Williams' symbolism of death a little heavy handed? Perhaps the playwright expects us to laugh. There is a hint of farce in this description, which ends with an irreverent tale about a revivalist, Gypsy Jones, condemning Episcopalian card parties.

The light **motif** runs right through the scene (see Lighting in Critical Approaches). It is used to link the characters and reveal their innermost feelings. When he sits down next to Laura, Jim complains

y

that he is 'in the limelight' (p. 292), something that he is quite comfortable with, despite his protestations. Does this confident egotism hint that Jim will be unable to help trampling all over the girl's feelings? Jim belongs in the light, as his photograph in *The Torch!* signifies, while Laura prefers the dark, which enables her to keep her secrets. *The Torch!* is aptly named, since the girl has been worshipping Jim's image for six years or more. Jim hopes to obtain a job in television in the future, while Laura enjoys watching the light playing on her glass figurines. Williams expects the reader to compare the modern, dynamic light source with static, old-fashioned ornaments. Which are we more drawn to? Televisions may not break 'if you breathe' (p. 300), but they lack charm.

Ultimately, the light motif is used to demonstrate the incompatibility of Laura and Jim, who, **ironically**, get along well together. Is Williams hinting that there might have been a genuine chance for Laura if the 'emissary from the world of reality' (Scene 1, p. 235) had not already met Betty 'on a moonlight boat trip up the river' (p. 306)? We cannot be sure. The romantic, flickering light of the candle Jim carries into the Wingfield living room is cancelled out by the more powerful and enduring light of the moon under which he met his fiancée. Williams' stage directions make it clear that knowledge of Jim's attachment to Betty deals Laura a blow from which she is unlikely to recover: *'the holy candles on the altar of* LAURA'*s face have been snuffed out'* (p. 307). In the last lines of the play Tom draws our attention to the fact that his sister doesn't belong in Jim's modern world of *'Knowledge – Zzzzzp! Money – Zzzzzp! – Power!'* (p. 300). She is out of place ' – for nowadays the world is lit by lightning!' (p. 313). Are these words regretful or bitter? Should the actor playing Tom deliver the instruction 'Blow out your candles, Laura –' (p. 313) in a sorrowful tone? Or is the narrator simply pleading for peace of mind? Tom's final references to light confirm the power of memory. The narrator associates light with Laura – as if she is something precious to him still. He cannot escape her and is 'pursued by something' all his life: 'I reach for a cigarette, I cross the street … anything that can blow your candles out!' (p. 313). The guilt will not go away.

The main business of the scene is to show the awakening and disillusionment of Laura. Williams' portrayal of the glass menagerie is central to our understanding of this, for Laura comes to life when she finds the confidence to talk about and share her hobby. When the girl first mentions her ornaments Jim is not quite sure what she is talking about. 'What did you say – about glass?' (p. 298) he asks. Instead of answering the question, Laura turns away shyly, not yet secure enough to discuss her consuming passion with her idol. Luckily, Jim has the sensitivity to change the subject, revealing his essential niceness. However, Laura returns to the topic a few minutes later, demonstrating a tenacity we might not have suspected she possessed. Jim is still confused, but asks a more focused question, 'I'm not right sure I know what you're talking about. What kind of glass is it?' (p. 300), which gives Laura an opening to speak at greater length.

Laura's trust in Jim has grown rapidly. She holds out her favourite figurine for him to hold, revealing a charming sense of humour as she talks about the unicorn and horses getting along 'nicely together … I haven't heard any arguments among them!' (p. 301). During this sequence, many of the characters' utterances are significant in ways that they are unaware of. There is a good deal of **pathos**. Jim says he is 'pretty clumsy with things' (p. 300) when Laura give him the unicorn to hold. After the dance he will break not just the ornament, but also her heart. Like the unicorn she favours and identifies with, the old-fashioned girl of a type all but 'extinct in the modern world' (p. 301) is 'lonesome' but 'doesn't complain' (p. 301). Most poignant of all is the extent to which Laura is enlivened by Jim's interest in her. The gentleman caller seems to be offering her the chance to reach beyond the narrow confines of her private world, something the reader will by now be convinced she secretly wants. Laura allows Jim to move her unicorn from the shelf he is kept on: 'Put him on the table. They all like a change of scenery once in a while!' (p. 301). The girl's gentle command is daring. Have we ever heard her tell someone to do something or express an interest in change? Up to this moment in the play Laura's whole purpose has been to keep herself secure in one spot. Now she is even able to participate in a 'clumsy waltz' (p. 302).

The reader will be aware that the dance is a temporary illusion of romance. The music is provided by the slightly seedy dance hall and Jim's invitation is couched in prosaic terms: 'How about cutting the rug a little, Miss Wingfield?' (p. 301). Nonetheless, we recognise the waltz is an opportunity for Laura to live like an ordinary, popular girl for a few moments. Jim's pantomime with the dance programme on p. 301 is significant: 'Let me have a look at it. [*Grasps imaginary card.*] Why, every dance is taken! I'll just have to scratch some out.' Is the boy's kindness really unwitting cruelty? Jim feeds Laura's romantic fantasies without knowing that he is doing it. Sadly, she is brought down to earth just at the moment when she begins to lose some of her self-consciousness and starts to enjoy herself: 'Ha-ha! … [*They suddenly bump into the table.* JIM *stops.*]'. This is the turning point in the scene, and in Laura's life. From now on until the end of the play, the girl is forced to confront reality head on.

How does Laura deal with this? Some critics argue that Laura is destroyed by the events of Scene 7, while others suggest she possesses inner resources that indicate that recovery might be possible. Laura is not overwhelmed by dismay when the unicorn's horn is knocked off: 'It doesn't matter. Maybe it's a blessing in disguise' (p. 303). This magnanimous response comes before she learns about Betty's existence. At this moment Laura still perhaps hopes that she can be 'less – freakish' (p. 303) and normal, like her favourite figurine. The truth dawns slowly. After she has been kissed, Laura fails to notice Jim's discomfort. She sits smiling on the sofa, ignoring the ritualistic offers of a cigarette or Life-Saver mint. Is she locked in her own dream world again? Her agony begins when Jim makes a series of negative statements, explaining why he can't call again: '*Slowly, very slowly,* LAURA'S *look changes, her eyes returning slowly from his to the ornament in her palm*' (p. 306). The first thing she did after she was kissed was to look at the glass unicorn; at the moment when '*the sky falls*' (p. 309), Laura's reaction is the same. Is this cruel proof that the girl was correct not to stray far from her ornaments? Will she ever be able to look into a young man's eyes again?

Probably not, although her ability to withdraw into herself allows Laura to preserve her dignity at a crucial moment. She asks a question *'faintly'* (p. 306) and then remains struggling *'with her storm'* (p. 307) on the sofa. A negative reading of these moments would suggest that Laura does not possess sufficient strength to remove herself from the scene of her distress, as was her impulse in Scene 6. If Laura is broken, how are we to interpret her decision to give Jim the damaged unicorn? Williams tells us that the girl has *'a look of almost infinite desolation'* (p. 307), a phrase which indicates that a great deal of damage has been done to her. However, the adverb 'almost' and the brave smile and lip biting that occur just before the brave girl places the unicorn into the palm of Jim's hand and *'pushes his fingers closed upon it'* (p. 307), prove that she is not completely annihilated. She may not be able to say more than two words, but Laura is quietly forceful in her gift-giving.

The next move that Laura makes is ambiguous. She gets up to wind the victrola. Is she retreating into the past again, or is this a healthy sign that she is capable of comforting herself? We cannot be sure. Williams does not refer to Laura again until Jim's exit, when she utters a single word – which is elicited from her by her mother – and shakes the caller's hand (p. 310). During the final argument between Tom and Amanda, Laura winds up the victrola but does not speak. Sadly, and perhaps appropriately, the last sound that comes from her lips is a scream, in response to Tom smashing his glass. Like this dramatic cry of pain, her final position, *'huddled upon the sofa'* (p. 312), suggests fear and defeat. But even now Williams allows us to feel there might be a little hope left for the wounded girl. In spite of her misery, Laura is able to lift her hair and 'smile at her mother' (p. 312) when she is soothed.

Will our sympathy for Laura prevent us from sympathising with the other characters? In spite of the terrible hurt that he causes, Jim is not portrayed as a villain. He is pompous and a little too caught up in himself to be fully aware of the effect he is having on Laura, but he also has a good heart. His psychological analysis of Laura's 'inferiority complex' (p. 298) and 'advice' (p. 299) about learning to believe in herself may be trite, but Jim is sincere. The problem is that Jim gets carried away by his own speeches and ends up 'way off beam' (p. 305). Jim has been told by a friend that he 'can analyse people better than doctors that make a profession of it' (p. 298). The devastating kiss occurs at the close of Jim's long 'diagnosis' of Laura, almost as if it is the logical 'therapeutic' outcome of his 'treatment'. But, of course, Jim is being unfair. A young man who is to be married in less than three months time has no business kissing other girls. To his credit, Jim realises this immediately.

Jim has other weaknesses and insecurities which make him easier to empathise with. The self-confidence he displays for much of Scene 7 is not armour-plated. Jim is truly abashed after he has kissed Laura, and unable to banter quite so skilfully with Amanda when she reappears. He sounds like a very ordinary and rather awkward boy as he offers his clichéd excuses to leave. Jim's admission that 'The cat's not out of the bag at the warehouse yet' (p. 310) indicates that he is not yet fully comfortable in his role as fiancé. Having the boss's ear is not enough to make him feel truly secure at the shoe company; he fears the mockery he'll receive from his co-workers. Like all the other characters, the gentleman caller is vulnerable. Jim differs from the Wingfields in one crucial respect, however. He has found a way to negotiate the external world. Jim is perhaps lucky that his dreams are mundane and conformist. He does not need to get lost at the movies or take refuge from reality in his imagination. Knowledge, money, power, 'the cycle democracy is built on!' (p. 300) are what inspire him. The flights of fancy we see him take in this scene – the pantomime with the dance card, going along with the quirky discussion about the menagerie – are interludes for Jim.

Although she is not on stage for most of the scene, Williams ensures that we are aware of Amanda throughout the encounter she has set up. Peals of her *girlish laughter* (pp. 300, 305) can be heard from the kitchen on two occasions; when Laura first mentions her glass collection to Jim, and then when the unicorn is broken. The timing of these outbursts is significant. It seems as if Laura is being unconsciously mocked and undermined. Interestingly, we learn that it is Amanda who calls the glass animals a 'menagerie', a much less dignified term than the more gracious 'collection', which is Laura's choice. The mother is now a suffocating presence. Her exuberance make her overbearing in her interactions with Jim. She ignores the serious looks on the young people's faces when she returns with a pitcher of punch, concentrating instead on her own rejuvenation and fun: 'I was so gay as a girl!' (p. 308). More painful still is her assumption that Jim will now come to visit 'all the time' (p. 309), when he is desperately trying to escape for ever. How will poor Laura feel, as she has to listen to another account of Jim's love affair, which has to be told for Amanda's benefit? It is difficult to sympathise with the mother when she turns on her son at the end of the scene, although we may understand her irritation. Amanda's use of plain language, which she has previously eschewed, shows us that she is finally facing the painful truth: 'Don't think about us, a mother deserted, an unmarried sister who's crippled and has no job!' (p. 312). Shortly after this desperate statement comes an insult. The mother's final line is an example of unconscious irony: 'Go, then! Then go to the moon – you selfish dreamer!' (p. 312), she yells at Tom. Amanda could be talking about herself. She is as much a selfish dreamer as her son. During the play both have wished on the moon, but failed to achieve the peace of mind that they longed for. In the closing moments Williams rehabilitates Amanda's character: *'Now that we cannot hear the mother's speech, her silliness is gone and she has dignity and tragic beauty'* (p. 312). This reminder that strong maternal love and devotion motivate Amanda's selfishness heightens the pathos and bleakness of the ending.

Screen images and legends and music are used to highlight and comment on moments of intense emotion in this scene. As in Scene 6, Laura is most often the focus. Sometimes, legends foreshadow an event or utterance; for example, 'SOUVENIR' appears on the screen before Laura gives Jim the unicorn, hinting that the girl mulls over the idea of giving a gift for some time. This suits her serious, contemplative nature. The early appearance of this legend also demonstrates that Laura has perhaps begun to retreat into the past even before she hears about Betty. Was the 'here and now' always going to be too much for her? The legend 'THE SKY FALLS' neatly encapsulates the girl's agony, while 'THINGS HAVE A WAY OF TURNING OUT SO BADLY!' is surely an ironic understatement. Why does the playwright introduce this darkly humorous note? Is he concerned that there has been too much **pathos** in Scene 7? Perhaps not. The final moments of the play are graceful, dignified and very sad. The silent pantomime brings us full circle. The play opened with a mimed meal. Now we are presented with a much more sorrowful ceremony. The visual image of mother and daughter, mutually reassuring one another with smiles and gestures, is touching. We do not need to be able to hear Amanda's voice to understand what she is saying. If the content of Tom's closing monologue comes as no surprise, his haunted words provide some sort of **closure**. It is not comforting for the reader to learn that Tom has failed to find contentment in his wandering life, but it is appropriate that his sweet-natured, unique sister should have inspired enduring affection.

For a detailed discussion of a section of this scene see Textual Analysis 3.

Moses the Old Testament patriarch who led the Jews from Egypt to Moab, within sight of the Promised Land
Benjamin Franklin an American statesman (1706–90), who was also an author and scientist, famous for his practical inventions. Franklin demonstrated that lighting was a form of electricity when he flew a kite in a storm
Mr Edison Thomas Alva Edison (1847–1931) was another famous American inventor; he invented the gramophone and the first incandescent lamp
The Wrigley Building located in Chicago and named after William Wrigley Jr, who invented chewing-gum
that Kraut-head an insult used to describe Americans of German origin
LA GOLONDRINA a popular song of the period which celebrates the fading of summer; 'golondrina' is Spanish for 'swallow', a bird which migrates at the end of summer
stumble-john an obsolete slang term which means 'blunderer'
that was way off the beam another slang expression which means 'to be off course'; Jim knows he has made a mistake
the shank of the evening early in the evening
jalopy an obsolete term for 'an old, battered vehicle'
I'll be jiggered a colloquial expression of surprise

PART THREE

C RITICAL APPROACHES

C HARACTERISATION

A MANDA

Critics have suggested Tennessee Williams' most distinctive contribution to American drama is his portrayal of Southern gentlewomen who have fallen on hard times or made tragic mistakes. Often these women have survived intense emotional experiences, which have led to a decline. Williams' heroines are forced to face up to challenging situations. If they fight hard enough, as Amanda does, they will endure and find the strength to move on.

The actress Laurette Taylor, who played Amanda in the original production of *The Glass Menagerie*, effectively stole the show. This will come as no surprise to the modern reader. The backward-looking Southern belle dominates the stage with her elegiac arias about Blue Mountain and ferocious campaign to secure and impress a gentleman caller. Amanda is rarely at a loss for words, and energetically takes on a number of roles in her pursuit of success for herself and her children. She may be confused and misguided, but she possesses courage and vitality.

The many versions of Amanda we are exposed to include the martyred mother with the '*sweet suffering stare*' (Scene 2, p. 242). This Amanda is scared, asking forlorn questions to which she tries to find answers. 'So what are we going to do the rest of our lives?' is a typical query (Scene 2, p. 245). No wonder she is worried. Having been abandoned, the little woman has been battling alone for years. She fights to hold her family together, saying: 'in these trying times we live in, all that we have to cling to is – each other ...' (Scene 4, p. 258), and knowing full well that 'the future becomes the present, the present the past, and the past turns into everlasting regret if you don't plan for it!' (Scene 5, p. 269) These sharp words are proof that the heroine has a practical streak. She knows all about economic necessity and making the best of things, as her enthusiastic transformation of the Wingfield apartment demonstrates. The new clothes and furnishings she bought were paid for with the money she earned as

y

telephone saleswoman. Amanda's habitual morning call of 'Rise and Shine!' signifies valour, and we have to admire this refusal to retreat. As we listen to her chiding Tom about his debilitating habits we sense that Amanda is driven by worthy motives. She does not want her son to end up a drunkard like his father, and secondly, believing that her children are 'unusual' and 'just *full* of natural endowments' (Scene 4, p. 258), she hopes Tom will make a success of his career. This is natural, and we will warm to Amanda when she displays maternal pride, even if she is over-optimistic about her children's prospects.

However, the mother's refusal to acknowledge that Tom and Laura must be allowed to forge their own identities and live life according to their own ideas, makes her partly responsible for their crises and failures. Amanda's old-fashioned, puritanical values drive Tom to distraction, eventually pushing him away. Williams makes it clear that the row in Scene 7 will be one of the last confrontations between mother and son. Even when he tries to conform, bringing home the gentleman caller Amanda longed for, Tom faces accusations and complaints: 'What a wonderful joke you played on us!' (Scene 7, p. 311), 'you've had us all make such fools of ourselves' (Scene 7, p. 312). Here the mother becomes the shrill, babbling old 'witch' Tom complained about so bitterly in Scene 3. His final, unequivocal threat comes as no surprise: 'The more you shout about my selfishness to me the quicker I'll go, and I won't go to the movies!' (Scene 7, p. 312). Unlike her son, because she is a penniless woman, Amanda will remain trapped in the apartment she has attempted to rule like a small kingdom. Her vigilance and censorship of reading matter at the meal table come to nothing. Perhaps Williams even intends us to view Amanda's conventionality as a reason to reject her. Would Tom have stayed, continuing to provide financial support, if his mother had not been so blinkered and intolerant?

Sadly, the consequences of the mother's stifling expectations are most devastating for Laura. The girl's heart is broken by the young man Tom brings home, and then her beloved brother absconds, leaving her alone with a mother who is part protectress, part victimiser. Williams makes use of dark **irony** in his portrait of the mother-daughter relationship in *The Glass Menagerie*. On the positive side, Amanda works tirelessly to make her daughter's future secure. She recognises that Laura will just drift along unless she takes her in hand. However, the mother is also a rigid egotist. Amanda expects Laura to succeed on *her* terms. Her obsessive plans and provisions become increasingly unrealistic as she tries to recreate Laura in her own image, forcing the girl into the role of 'pretty trap' that *she* found congenial. The audience will condemn the mother for her destructive foolishness; after all, she receives sufficient warning – from both her offspring – that her schemes are fatally flawed. In Scene 1 Laura humbly reminds Amanda that she is 'not popular like you were in Blue Mountain' (pp. 239–40), while Tom is more direct: 'Mother, you mustn't expect too much of Laura … Laura is different from other girls' (Scene 5, p. 271).

  Why is Amanda unable to see and accept the truth about her children? Why does she alienate and damage Tom and Laura when she is seeking to protect them? The answer lies in her relationship with her past. Amanda is paralysed by nostalgia, unwilling and unable to let go of her youth. This interferes with her ability to square up to reality. She enjoys mythologising her girlhood in Blue Mountain so much that she loses sight of the present, and consequently Tom and Laura, who are hemmed in by their mother's memories. The ultimate expression of this is Scene 6, where Amanda resurrects her old dress and sashays across the stage, reliving the night of the Governor's ball. Amanda perhaps believes that she is setting a good example for her daughter to follow when she meets Jim O'Connor, but the audience knows that Laura has become incidental. Even when she is not on stage in Scene 7, Amanda's triumphant offstage laughter interrupts the encounter between Jim and Laura. This is proof that she unconsciously feels the evening belongs to her. In the dismal moments after Jim has left, it becomes clear that Amanda is taking things very personally. She takes out her wrath on her children, snapping at Laura, 'I don't believe that I would play the victrola' (p. 311). Her choice of pronoun is significant. It sounds as if Amanda feels *she* has been insulted by Jim's engagement. Subsequently she tries to tug at Tom's heart strings by shouting, 'Don't think about us, a mother deserted, an unmarried sister who's crippled and has no job!' (p. 312). This plain speaking could not come at a worse time. Overwhelmed by self-pity, Amanda puts herself first and inflicts yet another wound on Laura. Ultimately, it is impossible not to feel that the legends of the Old South that obsess Amanda are a far greater cause for concern than her financial worries. Amanda is doomed to dissatisfaction because it is impossible to recreate the past. The mother's paralysis is partly responsible for the disintegration of her family.

  When we see Amanda act out the role of coquette, we see the power of the imagination at work. Amanda is a self-deceiving romantic. Her eulogies show that she is blind to the truth about her past. Her tales are far removed from the reality of the dingy Wingfield apartment, which Amanda struggles to gloss over with a rose-coloured lampshade, monogrammed table linen and chintz covers. When reality does break through, Amanda is usually brought up short by it. Almost every reference the heroine makes to her husband is punctuated by an exclamation mark – 'One thing your father had plenty of – was charm!' (Scene 2, p. 247) – or trails off – 'And then I – [*She stops in front of the picture ...*] met your father! Malaria fever and jonquils and then – this – boy ...' (Scene 6, p. 277). The brevity of the recollections suggests strong emotion. An extended, realistic assessment of Mr Wingfield's character would be too painful for Amanda. Her wounds still smart. So she distracts herself by trying to conjure up romance for her daughter. The futility of her plan is neatly underlined when Amanda wishes on the moon in Scene 5. By the end of the play we will realise that Amanda is trapped by her illusions, and that, as the defrocked priest, Shannon, in Williams' *Night of the Iguana*, says, 'The helpless can't help the helpless'.

The bleakness of the playwright's vision is offset by the last image we have of Amanda. In the **tableau vivant** the mother achieves what critics have suggested is a moment of grace when she comforts Laura. Williams insists on Amanda's dignity at this moment; her movements are '*slow and graceful*', and she achieves '*tragic beauty*' (Scene 7, p. 312), wringing a smile from her damaged child. Perhaps her soothing words and gestures prove that victims can help other victims. This is the kind of quiet heroism that the playwright values and celebrates in all his work. In the final assessment, the anachronistic, eccentric, deluded and infuriating Amanda is worthy of compassion.

LAURA

Commenting on his sister Rose, who was his inspiration for the character of Laura, Tennessee Williams said, 'she was the member of the family with whom I was most in sympathy'. This sympathy led the playwright to create a portrait of a strange girl, whose aloneness is deeply touching.

Laura's uniqueness is conveyed by the **symbols** that we come to associate with her: blue roses, the unicorn in her glass collection and the victrola. The colour blue signifies melancholy coldness, draining the passion from the conventional flower of love. The delicate Laura clearly will not be

able to cope with strong emotions. Unicorns, 'extinct in the modern world'
(Scene 6, p. 301), are symbols of peace – which Laura craves – and purity.
This is appropriate. Laura needs to remain uncontaminated by the outside
world if she is to survive. The menagerie itself is kept on a shelf, and, like
Laura, vulnerable when humans are clumsy and thoughtless. The girl's
preference for her father's worn out phonograph records over the hot swing
music of the Paradise Dance Hall, suggests that Laura is in need of a male
protector, and would like to live in an earlier era. Altogether, these symbols
are powerful reminders that Laura is an oddity who does not belong in the
modern world.

Does Laura choose her isolation willingly? Her limp is obviously not
her fault, but her acute sensitivity about what others see as a minor, 'hardly
noticeable' disability, has prompted Laura to withdraw. The pattern was set
in high school, where her leg-brace prevented her from forging
relationships with other students. Jim makes this clear when he says, 'As I
remember you sort of stuck by yourself' (Scene 7, p. 295). Laura was also
crippled by shyness, which she was unable to 'work out of gradually' like
other people (Scene 7, p. 295). Early failure seems to have completely
destroyed the girl's fragile self-esteem. Since high school Laura has drifted
along, her lonely existence punctuated by disastrous forays into the world
outside the apartment. A visit to Garfinkel's Delicatessen fills her with
trepidation, so it is no wonder she manages only a few days at the Rubicam
business school before breaking down completely. Laura's limp is another
symbol of her outsider status, and like the glass menagerie, she guards it
cautiously, fearing attack.

However, Tennessee Williams makes it clear that Laura enjoys life
on her own limited terms. She copes with her neurosis by suppressing
herself. This makes her feel safe. For Laura, the apartment is not a prison,
but a refuge. She has successfully carved out a niche for herself at home.
She takes her glass collection very seriously, washing and polishing it
carefully. She listens to the victrola, helps with domestic chores and loves
her mother and brother very much. Laura has her dreams and memories
for company. She is every bit as romantic as her garrulous mother, poring
over her copy of *The Torch!*.

The problem for Laura is that she is not allowed to remain in her
suspended state. Her mother, who does not want her to be an old maid,
pulls her out of the past and into the present. And as is the case with

Y

Amanda, when fantasy meets reality, disaster strikes. She *'nervously echoes'* her mother's laugh when Amanda playfully asks if the family are expecting any young men to call in Scene 1 (p. 239). Laura's assessment of herself is pessimistic but realistic. She is aware of her limitations and fully understands that she is not a 'pretty trap'. Does this make her, as E. R. Wood has suggested, 'too negative, too abject a victim'? (Tennessee Williams, *The Glass Menagerie*, introduction by E. R. Wood, p. xv; see Further Reading)

The cruel climax of the play occurs when the secret desires that Laura has sublimated into her glass collection are fully awakened by Jim. Laura manages her emotional confinement effectively, but is completely broken when her feelings are exposed. Although she manages to smile at her mother at the end of Scene 7, we know the girl's chances of recovery are slim. *'The holy candles in the altar of* LAURA'S *face'* are *'snuffed out'* when she learns of Jim's engagement to Betty (Scene 7, p. 307). Laura was right not to want to move from her spot. Unlike her mother, she knew that acting on her desires would be a mistake, and her moment of weakness is severely punished. Ultimately, Williams' portrayal of Laura proves, as the hero Val in *Orpheus Descending* says, 'We are all of us sentenced to solitary confinement in our own skins'. The playwright's most delicate heroine is irrevocably damaged when she responds to someone who deceives her into thinking otherwise.

Tom

Tom has two voices in *The Glass Menagerie*. You will find comments on his role as narrator in Dramatic Techniques. This section will offer an analysis of Tom as protagonist in his 'memory play'.

Critics have suggested that Tom Wingfield is a self-portrait of the dramatist as a young man. Certainly, many of the details that Williams includes in his characterisation of Tom were drawn from his own life: the hateful job at the shoe company with its $65 wage, the poetic ambitions pursued at night and in the warehouse washroom, the love of D. H. Lawrence and the movies (see Sources and Williams' Life and Works for further details).

One of Tom's most intriguing and significant speeches was perhaps inspired by Williams' father's name: Cornelius Coffin Williams. In Scene 4 the compulsive movie-goer comes in late and regales his sister with a des-

cription of a magic show. The highlight of his evening was watching Malvolio
the Magician get out of a coffin 'without removing one nail' (Scene 4, p.
255). Tom admires the magician's skill: 'There is a trick that would come in
handy for me – get out of this 2 by 4 situation!' (p. 255). These lines neatly
sum up the protagonist's dilemma in *The Glass Menagerie*: how can he
escape from his mother and sister without removing a nail, i.e. causing
pain? Malvolio's coffin **symbolises** the life-in-death that Tom experiences
in both the Wingfield apartment and the warehouse. But, since he doesn't
possess magical powers, getting himself out of his prison is a very tough
proposition. If we consider the link between the name of Malvolio's clever
trick and Williams' father, it is possible to feel that the dramatist intends us
to view escape ambivalently. As a young man, Williams felt a great deal of
antagonism towards his father, so perhaps the trick named after him is an
ironic warning, rather than a promise of liberation. This idea becomes
clearer if we consider the ways in which the dramatist portrays Tom's
family relationships and feelings.

Amanda and Laura have both been scarred by Mr Wingfield's
desertion. But how does Tom feel about being abandoned? The play does
not provide us with straightforward answers. Tom obviously dislikes having
to work at the shoe company in order to support his mother and sister, but
his resentment does not take the form of explicit complaints about his
father. At times, Tom seems to want to emulate him. He is unapologetic
about his drinking and late hours. He spins fantasies of an amoral and
unconventional lifestyle, either in the criminal underworld, or 'far-off' in
the South Sea Islands or on safari (see Scene 3, p. 252 and Scene 6, pp.
282–83). However, despite the fact that he is undoubtedly keen to find an
escape route, we cannot be sure that Tom admires the man who made it as
far as Mexico. He sounds disgusted – with himself and his father – when
he tells Jim he is just like Mr Wingfield: 'The bastard son of a bastard'
(Scene 6, p. 283). These words are followed by enigmatic remarks: 'See how
he grins? And he's been absent going on sixteen years!' (Scene 6, p. 283).
Our understanding of the father–son relationship may ultimately depend
upon the way these lines are delivered by the actor playing Tom, whose
tone at this point might be bitter or wistful.

Why does Tom want to follow in his faithless father's footsteps? It is
more than a question of simple wanderlust, which seems to have been one
of Mr Wingfield's motivations. The reader needs to decide whether it is

the apartment or the warehouse that is most damaging to the fledgling poet. Both are slowly sucking the life out of Tom. At home Amanda nags him about his drinking and movie-going, and she makes it impossible for Tom to pursue his writing. She urges him to stop smoking so that he can afford to attend night-school and improve his prospects. The shoe company is dehumanising, and Tom feels alienated there. During his conversations with his mother, Tom repeatedly expresses his desire for some adventure – and the repetitive, mind-numbing tasks he is called on to perform in his job are the antithesis of the life he craves. By Scene 6 a vicarious existence in a cinema seat is no longer enough to distract or satisfy him: 'I'm not patient ... I'm tired of the *movies* and I am *about to move!*' (Scene 6, p. 283).

But what does Tom hope to achieve when he leaves? Has he thought through the consequences of abandoning his job, his mother and his sister? Ironically, the protagonist seems to be swapping one institution for another when he joins the Merchant Marines. It is easy to see why Tom needs to escape from Amanda's clutches if he is to have any chance of forging his own identity, but his relationship with his sister is surely not so stifling. Williams' portrayal of the brother–sister bond makes Tom's departure from the family home problematic. It is clear Laura and Tom are close. Tom is protective towards his sister, and dislikes upsetting her. However, it is possible to feel that Laura is a burden for Tom. Certainly, Amanda keeps reminding him that it is his duty to support her: 'you've got to look out for your sister ... because she's young and dependent' (Scene 4, p. 261). Does Tom collude with his mother when she becomes obsessed with the idea of inviting a gentleman caller home because he wants to be free of this responsibility?

It is difficult to tell exactly what Tom feels about match-making for Laura. Even though he does what his mother asks, Tom is reluctant to play the role of Cupid. He doesn't mention he has a sister when he issues his invitation, and threatens to call the whole thing off unless Amanda stops fussing. Is it unfair, then, to hold him partly responsible for the fiasco that ensues? At the end of the play, Tom refuses to accept any blame when he walks out of the apartment, leaving his mother to comfort Laura. We are informed that he left home for good a short while later. The final narrative makes it clear that Tom failed to recognise the hold his sister had over him. Brother and sister are both wounded by Tom's departure.

Williams hints that the guilt Tom feels is unavoidable, perhaps even necessary. The playwright describes Tom thus: 'A poet with a job in a warehouse. His nature is not remorseless, but to escape from a trap he has to act without pity' (p. 228). In Williams' work, pain is the inevitable result of cruelty and the victimiser often becomes the victim. Elsewhere in his writings, Williams says that the poet is 'always a tragic antagonist', because he has to reject falseness and impurity. In *The Glass Menagerie*, Tom is engaged in a battle for his own spirit, and to achieve self-fulfilment he has to reject society and its conformist, materialistic values, represented by Amanda and her tales of Blue Mountain and 'plans and provisions'. Like the other poets in Williams' oeuvre – Jonathan Coffin (Nonno) in *Night of the Iguana* and Sebastian Venable in *Suddenly Last Summer* – Tom becomes a homeless wanderer. It seems that exile is the price the poet must pay for his sensibility. However, in this early play, the poet finds it a struggle to pursue his dreams. And Williams even suggests that he has failed in his quest. Wherever Tom goes, he finds he is very much his mother's son, backward looking and haunted by his memories. Some critics have suggested that the protagonist is trapped in a no man's land of his own making at the end of the play, and that the torture of the outsider never ends. The enigmatic Tom Wingfield may not be the central character in *The Glass Menagerie*, but he perhaps pays the highest price for his dreams. Tom's belief that the world outside the apartment can provide a place of refuge is as misguided as any of Amanda's schemes.

JIM

Tennessee Williams claimed that he found it impossible to create 'normal' characters. He also said, 'If you write a character that isn't ambiguous you are writing a false character, not a true one.' Bear these remarks in mind when analysing the portrayal of the gentleman caller, especially when scanning the cast list, which offers a deceptively simplistic summary of Jim's qualities. There is more to the 'nice, ordinary, young man' (p. 228) than meets the eye.

The playwright's portrait of Jim is **ironic**. To begin with, we must consider the gap between appearance and reality. The young man who arrives at the Wingfield apartment is neither a gentleman, nor, in the strictest sense, a caller. Jim is of working-class Irish descent, a clerk in a warehouse, not the aristocratic planter or son of a planter Amanda had her sights set on as a girl. And he does not accept the supper invitation with the intention of winning Laura's heart. Already engaged and therefore 'spoken for', Jim is unaware that his friend 'Shakespeare' has a sister. He is merely filling in time before he collects his fiancée from the Wabash train depot. Significantly, the man Amanda hopes to cast in the role of Prince Charming is not even a dashing lover when he discusses the girl he has chosen. Critics have suggested that the young man's clichéd speeches about 'the power of love' (Scene 7, p. 307) lack conviction, and it is easy to accept this judgement. Feeling awkward about 'Romeo and stuff like that' (Scene 7, p. 310), Jim has kept his engagement a secret at work. Amanda finds herself dragging information out of the embarrassed boy in Scene 7, while Jim tries to close down the conversation with monosyllabic replies:

AMANDA

    Betty? Betty? Who's – Betty!

[*There is an ominous cracking sound in the sky*]

JIM

    Oh, just a girl. The girl I go steady with!

The *'ominous cracking sound'* underlines the mother's disillusionment, reminding the reader how foolish she was to pin all her hopes on the decent but dull Mr O'Connor.

There are other gaps to be considered, too, all of which undermine Jim's status as romantic hero and saviour. The young man's early promise has not translated into adult success. In spite of his gifts, Jim has had problems adapting to life in the mercantile world. Having suffered from an inferiority complex, he has committed himself to a course of self-improvement. Ironically, the lead singer in *The Pirates of Penzance* finds himself on a public-speaking course with the intention of enhancing his 'social poise' (Scene 6, p. 281). Jim's charm and good looks are not impregnable. He glances in the mirror when he talks to Laura, suggesting that he needs reassurance, just as she does. Earlier in the scene he hinted that he knows his days of shining like a star are over. Making himself 'comfortable as a cow' on the floor, he urges Laura to move closer so that he is not alone in the 'limelight' (Scene 7, p. 292). By this point Tom's allusion to ordinary, serviceable 'white chinaware' when describing Jim (Scene 6, p. 273) seems highly appropriate.

But this is not where he wants to be. Like all the other characters, Jim O'Connor has his fantasies. He expects to obtain a job in television once he has made the 'right connexions' (Scene 7, p. 300). We know that Jim is deluded about the future because Tom's retrospective opening narrative is pessimistic. Here the narrator draws attention to wars, conflict and the way in which 'the huge middle class of America was matriculating in a school for the blind' (Scene 1, p. 234). To use a cliché that is in keeping with O'Connor's characteristic mode of speech, Jim, a blind man whose vision is faulty, cannot be expected to lead the blind. He is not Moses, and cannot deliver Amanda and Laura from the wilderness. We cannot even be sure that he can make his own dreams a reality.

The gap between appearance and reality becomes destructive when the warehouse clerk meets Laura. To begin with, it looks as if the young man's charm and kindness are having a positive effect on his companion. Jim is living up to Laura's fantasies about him. The encouragement he offers is generous, but Jim is too narcissistic to appreciate fully Laura's delicate sensibility. He sees she is damaged, but assumes that she can learn to think of herself as superior in some way, as he has. Caught up in his role as amateur psychologist, he makes a fatal error of judgement. As he grabs her hand, Jim is really focused on himself. He momentarily forgets that actions might have consequences that he cannot predict or control. And he has failed to tell Laura the whole truth about himself. This sin of omission leads some critics to brand Jim a huckster. This reading of his character is plausible if we consider a speech he makes in Scene 7: 'Laura, you know, if I had a sister like you, I'd do the same thing as Tom. I'd bring out fellows and – introduce her to them. The right type of boys of a type to – appreciate her' (p. 306). These lines confirm that Jim belongs in the real world. He knows how match-making works. Did he simply choose to ignore the ugly truth about Tom's and Amanda's machinations because he was seduced by his own eloquence? During his final moments in the apartment, Jim bears little resemblance to 'Superman', the figure he jokily aligned himself with when he carried a bottle of wine and candelabrum into the living room (Scene 7, p. 290). Keen to escape from the location in which he has exposed himself as a 'stumble-john' (Scene 7, p. 305), Jim tries to make amends for his blunder with polite but awkward chit-chat. But it is far too late. Arguably, the caller causes Laura more pain, as she is forced to take his hand and wish him well. We will be glad to see the young man go.

y

Perhaps we should not be too hard on Jim. He has his vulnerabilities. His clumsy words and actions are not inspired by malevolence. Like all the characters, he has the misfortune to be living in a cruel world where dreamers get hurt. At the end of *The Glass Menagerie* the gentleman caller has been humbled, like the mother whose fantasies he was unable to fulfil.

THEMES

MEMORY

What exactly does Tennessee Williams mean when he describes *The Glass Menagerie* as a 'memory play'? In the production notes he talks of using the stage to arrive at a 'penetrating and vivid expression of things as they are' (p. 229). Memory is an imaginative tool which can be used to express the truth. This is the point Tom Wingfield makes in his opening narration when he says he is the opposite of a stage magician. He may use illusion, he may be sentimental and subjective, but the tale that he tells will be honest.

So how does memory work in this play? Critics have suggested that by re-enacting his past, Tom is able to embrace the mother he scorned, blamed and rejected as a young man. He is also trying to lay to rest the ghost of his sister, whose memory has haunted him for so long. The final lines of the play might be a plea for release: 'I speak to the nearest stranger – anything that can blow your candles out! ... Blow out your candles, Laura – and so good-bye ...' (Scene 7, p. 313). When he asks his sister to blow out her candles, the narrator confirms the uncontrollable power of his own memories. Tom cannot extinguish the light himself. The other characters are also unable – and unwilling – to forget the past. Amanda lives on her memories, fighting to reconstruct them in the present. Laura clings to objects – her menagerie, the victrola – which suggest memories are her only comfort. When her idealised image of Jim is destroyed and she is brought out of her reverie for a few moments, she disintegrates. O'Connor likes having Tom at the warehouse because his acquaintance from high school is a reminder of his former glory.

We might feel that the characters' inability to forget the past hinders them, but the images of light that are used throughout the play suggest the playwright's ambivalence about memory. Tom argues that the world is

Tom is forced to translate cutting words into deeds if he is to be his own man. It takes him some time. In Scene 1 he grumbles about listening to his mother's talk, but submits. By Scene 3 he is less tolerant, and not content to sit on the sidelines. He tries to replace his mother's fantasies of the South with a vision of a violent underworld. His sharp words suggest he is preparing for action. In Scene 6 he says he is ready to move, proving that he has taken his first step on the road to freedom by using the money to pay the light bill to join the Seaman's Union. But Tom is no action hero. He continues to bide his time at the movies. When he does go, he continues to look back with regret. Does the playwright undercut the protagonist by having him leave St Louis after he is fired? Perhaps liberation is always partly ignominious retreat in Williams' world.

DESIRE

In his first play Williams does not deal with sexual themes directly, as he will in later works. Desire is nevertheless an important concern. Ruby Cohn suggests that the characters in *The Glass Menagerie* sublimate their animal drives into aesthetics (see Further Reading). Laura focuses on her glass collection, Tom has his movies, poems and the writings of D. H. Lawrence. Amanda lingers over her romantic memories, while Jim is preoccupied by clichéd dreams about 'making it big'.

We might ask why the cast are so scared of passion. And why is the playwright reluctant to make them desiring subjects? Williams perhaps provided an answer when he said, 'I've always felt … that human relations are terrifyingly ambiguous.' He also commented, 'All my life I have been haunted by the obsession that to desire a thing or to love a thing intensely is to place yourself in a vulnerable position, to be a possible, if not a probable, loser of what you most want' (see Introduction to *Sweet Bird of Youth*, p. 10). *The Glass Menagerie* is a play in which characters are afraid to cross thresholds of any kind. Bold expressions of desire are simply too risky for the timid people we see here. The playwright also insists repeatedly that romance is a deceptive illusion. Amanda found this out the hard way, so her son and daughter can be forgiven for not wanting to follow in her footsteps.

Williams' portrayal of human relationships is essentially pessimistic. Laura and Jim share a few moments of true empathy, but then the door closes and they are alone again. At the end of *The Glass Menagerie* desire has proved to be a destructive and humiliating force.

FRAGILITY

If the playwright refuses to celebrate love and desire, how does he feel about human frailty? This is territory with which Tennessee Williams is comfortable. Early in his career he commented, 'I can't expose a human weakness on stage unless I know it through having it myself.' Williams made it his business to explore the inner lives of individuals who felt emotionally or socially traumatised. He pits the delicate against the brutal, the pure against the corrupt. In this play he aims to show us the plight of the dispossessed. In *The Glass Menagerie* all of the characters suffer a loss of self-confidence as they struggle to survive in a hostile environment. Even Jim is not immune from needing reassurance. Jim values the 'right connexions', believing that they will help him leapfrog his way to the top. The Wingfields rely on one another, and they are more fragile still. Amanda is distraught when she thinks that she has made herself a hateful witch to her children. Tom feels wretched when he upsets Laura. And Laura is simply too paralysed by inadequacy to step outside the apartment.

Although he is aiming at **pathos**, Williams does not want his audience to dismiss his characters as pathetic losers. Instead he wants us to see the heroism of the sensitive and solitary individual. He does this by focusing on the way in which people endure against the odds.

ENDURANCE

Life is hard in *The Glass Menagerie*; as Amanda says, it calls for 'Spartan endurance!' (Scene 4, p. 259). We watch the Wingfields struggle against emotional and physical confinement, seeking ways of dealing with necessity. The playwright does not provide his characters with solutions to their problems, but he does suggest they possess positive qualities that can help them to carry on. Writing about Amanda, Williams said, 'the mother's valor is the core of *The Glass Menagerie* ... she's confused ... even stupid, but everything has got to be all right. She fights to make it that way in the only way she knows how' (*Conversations with Tennessee Williams*, ed. Albert J. Devlin, p. 14). Amanda may not triumph, and her reasoning may be flawed, but the little woman knows she must battle on if she and Laura are to survive. At the end of the play the mother achieves a kind of dignity when she comforts her daughter. It is even possible to argue that the broken Laura will endure; in her darkest moments she finds it in her heart to smile at the woman who has caused her so much pain.

These small acts of human compassion are typical of Williams' work, in which tenderness and generosity are celebrated. The world of *The Glass Menagerie* would be intolerable if individuals were unable to huddle together for comfort once in a while. Endurance is made possible by moments of grace. The characters are at their best when they try to respond to each other's needs, even if they make mistakes. Tom and Laura tolerate Amanda's elegy about Blue Mountain because, as Laura says 'she loves to tell it' (Scene 1, p. 237). This is indulgence, but what alternative is there? Amanda becomes frantic when she is faced with ugly truths. Tom apologises to his mother in Scene 4, not because he didn't mean what he said in Scene 3, but because he recognises her devotion. It infuriates him, but he salutes it. When he is cruel, it is necessary for his own survival, not because he enjoys hurting others. Jim tells Laura he will treasure the souvenir she has given him in Scene 7 because he knows her glass collection is important to her, and because he vainly hopes to make amends for being a 'stumble-john'. Like Tom, the caller is regretful when he causes harm. Guilt seems to be a universal condition in Williams' work, but it is proof of affection.

DRAMATIC TECHNIQUES

Commenting on his approach to writing for the theatre, Tennessee Williams claimed that he had 'evolved a new method ... I call it the "sculptural drama" ... I visualized it as a reduced mobility on stage, the forming of statuesque attitudes or tableaux, something resembling a restrained type of dance, with motions honed down to only the essential or significant.' Essentially, Williams was aiming at 'stage poetry'. His new method set this play apart from the **naturalistic** dramas that dominated the American stage at the beginning of Williams' career. *The Glass Menagerie* may be a quiet and restrained piece, but its theatricality is sophisticated. The playwright uses a number of techniques – many of them experimental – to ensure that his audience is engaged by the seemingly uneventful lives he portrays.

SETTING

Tennessee Williams' descriptions of the stage setting for *The Glass Menagerie* are precise and detailed (see pp. 233–234). However, he was aiming not at straightforward **realism**, but at achieving a rather dreamlike interior. We are not given the impression that the fourth wall of the Wingfield apartment is missing. Instead, Williams draws attention to the artifice of the theatre by introducing gauze scrims, which are raised and lowered during the play. The shifting walls reflect one of the play's main themes: the elusive quality of memory. When he asks us to peer through the gauze, Williams reminds us that we are being taken back in time and made to look at something from a particular point of view. Thus Williams is able to hint at the subjectivity of the narrator.

Williams uses his single setting to emphasise the confinement of his characters' lives. During the seven scenes of the play, characters make entrances and exits, and allude to other places. The dance hall in particular is associated with temporary and deceptive illusions, making us suspicious of the world outside the apartment. This is appropriate. When he is allowed to work in it, the apartment is a refuge for Tom, as it is for Laura.

The wider world remains insubstantial, too. We begin to get the feeling that escape is impossible; Europe is consumed by war, America is afflicted by labour disturbances. The poet's fantasies are exotic but vague; he mentions the South Sea Islands and safaris but we never discover exactly where it is he runs to. Because he traps them in one domestic setting, eschewing elaborate spectacle, Williams is able to focus closely on the characters' inner lives and concerns.

Williams' primary concern – psychological realism – is conveyed by his use of one particular feature of the setting, the fire-escape. This seemingly naturalistic part of the set is actually symbolic. Tom tries to elude his mother's demands by smoking here. He also makes his forays to the movies via the fire-escape. In Scene 5 the Wingfields go outside to make their wishes on the moon. The fire-escape is the place where dreaming happens. But this location proves to be as deceptive as the Paradise Dance Hall.

Laura is in danger when she leaves the apartment, stumbling when she goes out on to the stairs in Scene 4. More significantly, Tom is drawn back inexorably to St Louis, and to his place of retreat, because he is haunted by Laura. He delivers his commentaries from the fire-escape, proving that it wasn't actually an escape-route after all.

THE SCREEN DEVICE

The Screen Device is the most controversial theatrical effect used in *The Glass Menagerie*. Magic lantern slides bearing images and titles were intended to be cast on a section of wall between the front room and the dining room areas, suggesting that they were central to the playwright's dramatic conception. However, they were abandoned in the original production because the play's director did not like them. When the play was published, Williams restored the images and legends, believing that they 'give accent to certain values in each scene'. Concerned that the episodic structure of the play might prevent the audience from being able to follow the narrative line, Williams also felt that the screen device held an 'emotional appeal' (p. 230). Critics remain divided. Some complain that the images and legends are too whimsical, and that they undermine or detract from the **pathos** of the play. In particular, critics worry that Laura's plight is trivialised and ridiculed.

The question of whether or not the screen device is intrusive deserves careful consideration. A reader of the play can arrive at a satisfactory interpretation of Williams' dramatic intentions, but can only guess at the effects of the legends and images in the theatre. There are almost forty projections altogether, and in some scenes they are shown in quick succession. They are heavily used at moments of tension and intensity. Is this distracting in a play which focuses on deeply felt emotions? A number of critics have argued that the characters are presented in an essentially naturalistic style, which is at odds with the **expressionistic** and alienating screen device, which keeps the audience at a distance.

Finally, the reader needs to consider the screen device in relation to the dramatist's use of setting, music and lighting, all of which are intended to create an impression of dreamlike insubstantiality. By using flashing images on a screen, Tennessee Williams is drawing attention to the way in which memory works.

Music

Tennessee Williams' imaginative use of music is highly effective. In his production notes, the playwright included detailed comments about 'The Glass Menagerie' theme, which 'is primarily Laura's music' (p. 231). The single recurring tune, which is sad, delicate and light, is supposed to 'give emotional emphasis to suitable passages'. The cinematic use of a repeated theme is also intended to serve as 'a thread of connexion and allusion between the narrator with his separate time and space and the subject of his story'. The linking of Tom and Laura through the use of music serves two purposes. Firstly, it is suggestive of the strong emotional bond that exists between brother and sister. Secondly, the music is used to bridge the spheres of time. This is highly appropriate in a play which is constructed to reflect the movements of the narrator's mind.

'The Glass Menagerie' theme is first played during the opening narration. The tune accompanies Tom's introduction to the characters who will appear in his memory play. Right from the start, we realise that the theme is designed to draw attention to significant moments in the characters' lives. It is heard in every scene. On almost every occasion, it is directly associated with something that is happening to, or being said about, Laura. For example, in Scene 1 it plays faintly when Laura leaves the room after the painful discussion about receiving gentleman callers, continuing through the end of the scene and into Scene 2. It is still playing when Amanda enquires whether her daughter has ever liked a boy. In Scene 6 the heart-rending legend, THIS IS MY SISTER, CELEBRATE HER WITH STRINGS! is complimented by music. The theme makes it plain that we should continue to focus on Laura, in spite of her mother's spirited scene-stealing with an old frock and bunch of jonquils. Perhaps the most poignant use of 'The Glass Menagerie' tune occurs in Scene 7, when Jim and Laura handle the glass unicorn, prior to their waltz. This is the final appearance that the theme makes, perhaps underlining the fact that life is over for Laura when her unicorn is shattered.

There are several other more **naturalistic** or conventional sources of music which help Williams to create mood. A key off-stage source is the Paradise Dance Hall, from which sensuous hot swing, waltzes and tangos emanate. We know that Laura is out of her element – and consequently in trouble – when Jim asks her to dance to a Mexican waltz, 'La Golondria', which is playing across the alley. It comes as no surprise that she attempts to block out the music that accompanies her disillusionment by moving towards the victrola when she gets a chance (see p. 307).

Tango music is as threatening as the Mexican waltz. In Scene 5 Tom tries to get his mother to face the fact that Laura is peculiar. In the middle of the conversation, the dance hall music changes to a tango '(THAT HAS A MINOR AND SOMEWHAT OMINOUS TONE)'. We know that Amanda's blindness will precipitate a fiasco. Amusingly, the music undermines the foolish mother in Scene 7, when the band at the Paradise Dance Hall *'goes into a tender waltz'* (p. 309) while Jim tells Amanda about the girl he goes steady with. This is the very last tune the humiliated woman would probably choose to hear at this moment. Williams picks this romantic waltz for another reason. It poignantly emphasises Laura's loss, as does the final use of music in the play. When Tom violently smashes his glass on the floor and plunges out to the fire-escape, the dance-hall music goes up, punctuated by a scream from Laura. This is a highly appropriate climax to a play which is a text-book example of how to use music evocatively at just the right moment.

LIGHTING

The production notes make it plain that Williams uses the lighting to draw our attention to themes and characters in very specific ways. The stage is dim because this is 'in keeping with the atmosphere of memory' (p. 231). More importantly, the clear pools of light that are designed to fall most often on Laura will be noticeable in a dusky setting, focusing our attention on the girl, even when she is not speaking. In Scene 3, while Amanda and Tom quarrel, Laura's figure is highlighted. The girl's silent agony is as significant as her mother's and brother's exasperation. This use of lighting foreshadows the supper scene, when Laura will sit huddled on a sofa, visible but not participating. Scenes 6 and 7 are the most trying scenes for Laura, and the lighting ensures that we remember this.

There are a number of sources of, and references to, light that inform our understanding of the play. The neon lights of the Paradise Dance Hall are garish **symbols** of the modern world in which the Wingfields are uncomfortable. The 'delicate rainbow colours' of the chandeliers (Scene 5, p. 265) provide an atmosphere of fake romance. Amanda's rose-coloured

Y

shade is attractive, but the mother makes a futile gesture when she buys it. Even the moon, a potentially powerful source of natural light, seems fragile. It is only a 'little silver slipper of a moon' (Scene 5, p. 266) and it rises over Garfinkel's Delicatessen. When the lights go out at the beginning of Scene 7 we recognise that harsh reality cannot be kept at bay any longer. Significantly, this failure occurs because Tom deliberately used the bill money to join a union.

Scene 7 takes place by candlelight. Because candlelight is so easily extinguished, we know that the moments of elation Laura enjoys will be fleeting. This point is underlined by the unrealistic way in which Mr Wingfield's portrait is lit up at different times during the play. Amanda's marital happiness was short-lived, just as her daughter's romance with Jim will be. The grinning photograph on the wall is a permanent reminder of the foolishness of trusting in appearances. Williams' use of light is often **expressionistic**. A spot of light on Amanda in Scene 1 helps suggest the power of the mother's memories. In Scene 3 the quarrel takes place in a 'turgid smoky red glow' which sounds decidedly threatening (p. 250). 'Gesticulating shadows are cast on the ceiling' (p. 250), adding to the impression of violence that the playwright wants to create. At the beginning of Scene 5 all the Wingfields seem fragile as they move about on the stage, 'as pale and silent as moths' (p. 264). In Scene 6 Laura's delicate beauty is emphasised by the *'lemony light'* in the apartment (p. 274). Here the lighting is used to provide a *'momentary radiance'* which suggests that the girl *'is like a piece of translucent glass'* (p. 274).

THE NARRATOR

Williams' use of a narrator who also participates in the story he tells enables the playwright to draw attention to the theatricality of *The Glass Menagerie*. Tom claims that he is not a stage magician, but he is director of the drama that unfolds. He chooses when the characters will enter, and introduces them. The play's episodic structure reflects the way his mind works, and the events that we see are those he chooses to show us. Lighting and music are sentimental because this suits Tom's conception of memory.

Tom's first job as narrator–dramatist is to provide the audience with background information about the historical setting. The brief **prologue** establishes the mood and tone, and introduces an important theme: the fight to survive. The truth of the tale Tom is to tell is guaranteed because he is an eye-witness. Since the play is not **naturalistic** in a traditional way, we will not be overly concerned by the inclusion of conversations and events at which the narrator was not present. In the theatre, the inconsistency of Scenes 2 and 6 goes unnoticed. Besides, Tom presents the emotional and imaginative truth through reconstruction.

By the end of the first narration the audience will have picked up on two of the narrator's key functions: to frame the action, and to offer a commentary on it. But Tom is no Greek chorus. It does not take us long to realise that he is deeply affected by the tale he tells. The **ironic** detachment that characterises some of his pronouncements perhaps covers up anguish and disappointment, although Tom is never self-pitying. Tom's two voices enable us to see events and characters from different perspectives. When he observes from the fire-escape, Tom seems to have achieved a reasonably comfortable distance, but before long we see him acting out the role of angry son again. When we listen to the narrator we are simultaneously pushed away from the action and drawn closer to it. This helps Williams to achieve the melancholy, reflective tone that he seeks. The playwright does not allow his narrator to overwhelm the drama. Although Tom's values and perceptions shape the way we respond to the characters, the playwright puts each individual at centre stage at some point. *The Glass Menagerie* is not just Tom's story.

STRUCTURE

The play consists of seven scenes – which are not equal in length – and four allusive narratives. The opening and closing scenes are framed by narratives which bear some resemblance to the traditional **prologue** and **epilogue**, but here the resemblance to the traditional well-made play ends. Tennessee Williams is not interested in observing the dramatic unities because he is aiming at psychological realism rather than **naturalism**. This is why the opening and closing scenes include silent pantomimes, which are deliberately theatrical in an **expressionistic** way. The seemingly casual, loose structure the playwright uses is intended to mirror the way in which the narrator's memory works. Moreover, the handling of time suggests that past, present and future are fluid and inter-related in *The Glass Menagerie*. Tom begins and ends the play by looking back in time. He steps out of time

y

to deliver his narratives about Amanda and Jim in Scenes 3 and 6. He skips time when it suits him, focusing on key moments in his story, rather than offering a straightforward, objective, linear account. The structure encourages us to believe that we are being offered snapshots of the truth, or truths.

There are three distinct periods of time that Williams bridges through his use of a narrator: the Second World War, in which we assume Tom served as a merchant seaman, the Depression, during which the main action takes place, and Amanda's girlhood in the rural South before the First World War. Are any of these periods a time of optimism? Emphatically, no. Even Blue Mountain is a place of violence. By linking these periods through Tom, Williams is able to suggest that the cycles of history will continue to trap humanity. The treatment of time compliments the dramatist's refusal to provide **closure** at the end of *The Glass Menagerie*.

We cannot even be sure where the climax of this episodic play occurs. Because the playwright does not move steadily towards a single dramatic climax, we have time to consider the route. A series of crises occur, but suspense does not play a large part in the proceedings. We know what the outcome will be from Scene 1 onwards. Our interest will therefore lie in listening to how the characters respond to events, and to each other. Certainly, nothing is resolved at the end of Scene 7. Tom has made his confession and celebrated his sister, but he remains rootless and haunted. We are not told what happened to Amanda, Laura or Jim after the fateful visit. Perhaps the final pantomime simply suggests a wheel has turned, and that Tom is back where he started when the family mimed their meal in Scene 1. His 'memory play' has not helped him move on. This is appropriate, since one of the messages of the play is that humanity is inexorably drawn to look back and go over the same ground, again and again. Critics have also suggested that Williams constructs his plays around a guilty secret which is never fully divulged. The small secrets that are kept are all damaging when they are divulged. The destructive role these small secrets play increase the bleakness of the vision presented in *The Glass Menagerie*.

IMAGERY AND SYMBOLISM

Like his narrator, Tennessee Williams has a poet's 'weakness for symbols' (Scene 1, p. 235). Laura's glass menagerie is the most important **symbol** in the play. It represents the fragility not just of the girl, but of all the characters. Laura sublimates her desire in the animals. She loves and protects them as if they were her children, or a husband. For Laura, they are an outlet. The exotic, extinct unicorn is her favourite creature, and she has had this figurine since she was a child. It is significant that Laura only has one unicorn, just as she only has one heart. Both are easily broken. When she allows Jim to handle the unicorn, we recognise the enormity of the occasion for Laura. She is inviting someone into her life, but the accident that occurs is not wholly Jim's fault. The girl enjoys waltzing, and is even able to view the situation with **ironic** detachment for a few moments. Is Williams suggesting that Laura secretly longs to be set free from the world of glass she has encased herself in? That she no longer wants to be a freakish, lonely creature herself?

Amanda is frustrated by the menagerie. For her, it is a symbol of her daughter's failure. She draws attention to it in a depressing speech in Scene 2, linking the glass collection to ideas about dependency and being 'stuck away in some little mousetrap of a room … eating the crust of humility' (Scene 2, p. 245). Tom recognises his sister's peculiarities but has more respect for the menagerie – and his sister's feelings – than Amanda. When his coat inadvertently strikes the shelf the glass collection is kept on at the end of Scene 3, he knows he has wounded Laura. This accident foreshadows the more serious maiming that will occur in Scene 7. Jim expresses interest in the glass menagerie when he is talking to Laura, proof that he has benign intentions at the beginning of their encounter. Later, he seems genuinely concerned when the unicorn is broken. He claims he will treasure it as a souvenir when he leaves. Will we be surprised when Laura gives up her favourite? Probably not. Laura gave Jim her heart long before she met him, and it seems fitting that she should abandon the painful reminder of her intense emotions when her idol departs. The menagerie without the unicorn represents Laura as she is at the end of the play: incomplete and broken. The glass menagerie also symbolises all the hopeless dreams that have preoccupied the characters during the play.

The mirror and photographic portrait in the apartment can be linked to the glass collection. Both are symbols of insecurity, and they make the audience uneasy. Jim glances into the mirror and adjusts his tie when he is talking to Laura. The boy is not as self-assured as he seems, and a little narcissistic. Jim's gestures suggest that he is capable of making unconscious mistakes because he is self-absorbed. The grinning portrait of Mr

Wingfield is a permanent reminder that love cannot be counted on. The telephone in the apartment is another symbol of deception: Mr Wingfield worked for the telephone company before he tripped the light fantastic out of town.

The most deceptive romantic symbol in the play is the gentleman caller. In Scene 1 much is made of the legendary afternoon when seventeen young men came calling. Amanda is not allowed to linger over her triumph for long, however. Tom asks his mother cheeky questions when she describes her beaux; the sadness and violence that characterise the callers' later lives overshadows the romance of one brief afternoon. In the opening narration Tom describes the caller as 'the long-delayed but always expected something that we live for' (Scene 1, p. 235). By definition, the caller will never arrive. He is delayed, he is expected, people yearn for him, but they cannot know when or where he will turn up, if he turns up at all. Scene 5 opens with the hopeful legend 'ANNUNCIATION'. But any optimism we might feel is short-lived. The 'real' gentleman caller is a homely boy who doesn't know Laura exists. How absurd of Amanda to pin her hopes of financial and emotional salvation on a shipping clerk who earns $85 a month! Two of Amanda's meaningless catchphrases further undermine the idea of salvation. 'Rise and Shine!' is used to get Tom out of bed so that he can go to his hateful job at the warehouse, and 'You're a Christian martyr' is designed to entice callers into subscribing to a glamour magazine.

Finally, there is Jim's fatal kiss, which should be considered in relation to Laura's comment that glass breaks if you breathe. Kisses are traditionally symbols of romance, but in *The Glass Menagerie* we witness a kiss that symbolises death rather than life. Laura is awakened by Jim's kiss in the expected way, but because her unicorn has already been shattered, we know that this awakening is undesirable and dangerous.

PART FOUR

TEXTUAL ANALYSIS

TEXT 1   SCENE 3, PAGES 250–52

Tom explodes with frustration when Amanda disturbs his creative labours

[AMANDA'*s hair is in metal curlers and she wears a very old bathrobe, much too large for her slight figure, a relic of the faithless Mr Wingfield. An upright typewriter and a wild disarray of manuscripts are on the drop-leaf table. The quarrel was probably precipitated by* AMANDA'*s interruption of his creative labour. A chair lying overthrown on the floor. Their gesticulating shadows are cast on the ceiling by the fiery glow.*]

AMANDA

You *will* hear more, you –

TOM

No, I won't hear more, I'm going out!

AMANDA

You come right back in –

TOM

Out, out, out! Because I'm –

AMANDA

Come back here, Tom Wingfield! I'm not through talking to you!

TOM

Oh, go –

LAURA [*desperately*]

– Tom!

AMANDA

You're going to listen, and no more insolence from you! I'm at the end of my patience!

[*He comes back toward her.*]

TOM

What do you think I'm at? Aren't I supposed to have any patience to reach the end of, Mother? I know, I know. It seems unimportant to you, what I'm *doing* – what I *want* to do – having a little *difference* between them! You don't think that –

AMANDA

I think you've been doing things that you're ashamed of. That's why you act like this. I don't believe that you go every night to the movies. Nobody goes to the movies night after night. Nobody in their right mind goes to the movies as often as you pretend to. People don't go to the movies at nearly midnight, and movies don't let out at two a.m. Come in stumbling. Muttering to yourself like a maniac! You get three hours' sleep and then go to work. Oh, I can picture the way you're doing down there. Moping, doping, because you're in no condition.

TOM [*wildly*]

No, I'm in no condition!

AMANDA

What right have you got to jeopardize your job? Jeopardize the security of us all? How do you think we'd manage if you were –

TOM

Listen! You think I'm crazy about the *warehouse*? [*He bends fiercely toward her slight figure.*] You think I'm in love with the Continental Shoemakers? You think I want to spend fifty-five *years* down there in that – *celotex interior*! With – *fluorescent – tubes!* Look! I'd rather somebody picked up a crowbar and battered out my brains – than go back mornings! I *go!* Every time you come in yelling that God damn 'Rise and Shine!' 'Rise and Shine!' I say to myself, 'How *lucky dead* people are!' But I get up. I *go!* For sixty-five dollars a month I give up all that I dream of doing and being *ever!* And you say self – *selfs'* all I ever think of. Why, listen, if self is what I thought of, Mother, I'd be where he is – GONE! [*Pointing to father's picture.*] As far as the system of transportation reaches! [*He starts past her. She grabs his arm.*] Don't grab at me, Mother!

AMANDA

Where are you going?

TOM

I'm going to the *movies!*

AMANDA

I don't believe that lie!

TOM [*crouching toward her, overtowering her tiny figure. She backs away, gasping*]

I'm going to opium dens! Yes, opium dens, dens of vice and criminals' hang-outs, Mother. I've joined the Hogan gang, I'm a hired assassin, I carry a tommy-gun in a violin case! I run a string of cat-houses in the Valley! They call me Killer, Killer Wingfield, I'm leading a double-life, a simple, honest warehouse worker by day, by night a dynamic *tsar* of the *underworld, Mother.* I go to gambling casinos, I spin

away fortunes on the roulette table! I wear a patch over one eye and a false
moustache, sometimes I put on green whiskers. On those occasions they call me –
El Diablo! Oh, I could tell you things to make you sleepless! My enemies plan to
dynamite this place. They're going to blow us all sky-high some night! I'll be glad,
very happy, and so will you! You'll go up, up on a broomstick, over Blue Mountain
with seventeen gentlemen callers! You ugly – babbling old – *witch.* ...

In Scene 3 Tom is driven to speak out forcefully when his mother intrudes
on his territory. Up to this point he has contented himself with short
outbursts or asides to Laura, but Amanda's refusal to allow him any space
of his own – physical or mental – causes the most significant row we have
witnessed so far. In this brief scene, the playwright vividly conveys the
depth of Tom's frustration.

Tom loses control because of the difference between 'what I'm *doing*'
and 'what I *want* to do'. His detestation of his job comes across strongly in the
almost hysterical description he gives of life at Continental Shoemakers. Tom
tries to confront Amanda with the truth about his daily misery with sarcastic
rhetorical questions; 'You think I want to spend fifty-five years down there in
that – *celotex interior*! With – *fluorescent* – *tubes!*' The disjointed syntax suggests
a mind that is whirling. The frantic commands have the same sense of
urgency: 'Listen!', 'Look!'. The **imagery** Tom employs becomes increasingly
disturbing as he exaggerates to get his point across: 'I'd rather somebody
picked up a crowbar and battered out my brains – than go back mornings!', 'I
say to myself, "How lucky dead people are!"'. Spiteful negativity of this kind is
rare in *The Glass Menagerie*. Truly, Tom is at the end of his rope. And if he has
to suffer, he wants someone else to face the truth, too.

In his agitation he is rude and hurtful to Amanda. Before the speech
about the warehouse, it is highly likely that Tom is cut off in the middle of
telling her to go to hell ('Oh, go –'). Not even his sister's desperate plea for
calm can stop the torrent of cruel words. He swears at Amanda,
threatening to follow in his father's footsteps. He wants to go as 'far as the
system of transportation reaches!'. This line neatly sums up Tom's rejection
of his mother and her 'Rise and Shine' values. Tom is physically as well as
verbally threatening, crouching toward and overtowering Amanda's tiny
figure as he launches into another tirade, which is designed to silence his
mother with its ugliness. The impression of violence that has been
established is reinforced when Tom spins his wild fantasy about living a life

of crime. We can be sure that the talk of opium dens and criminals' hang-outs is genuinely alarming to Amanda, a conservative woman who prefers to ignore the seamier side of life. Tom's tales of the underworld are gleaned from the movies he watches so compulsively. He gets carried away as he tries on different, equally absurd, personalities for size – hoodlum, assassin, pimp. But there is truth in his craziness, and this is a play which takes one man's need to invent and reinvent his own personality seriously. Tom has been leading a double-life, just not the dubious sort of double-life his mother worries about. By day Tom is a simple, honest warehouse worker. By night he is a poet. And when he is not allowed to lead the life his imagination demands, he lashes out. Sadly, Amanda is unable to respect her son's true vocation, and this is why Tom punishes her with a revenge fantasy of himself as criminal mastermind. He knows that Amanda fears that he will turn into a wandering rascal like his father, and the hoodlum living an immoral life he conjures up here is an extreme example of the type that has caused Amanda so much misery. Will we condemn Tom for his excess?

Irony helps to lighten the tone of what can be a shocking spectacle: menacing son turning on fragile mother. The poetic gifts Tom takes so seriously are employed to ridicule and then insult an adversary who possesses very little real power. Williams has ensured that Amanda looks vulnerable in this scene by dressing her in metal curlers and a very old bathrobe which is a relic of her faithless husband. The final lines of Tom's long speech are cutting but essentially childish: 'You'll go up, up on a broomstick, over Blue Mountain with seventeen gentlemen callers! You ugly – babbling old – *witch* …'. Coming from a loved one, these words are certainly effective. They undermine Amanda's cherished vision of herself as successful Southern belle. However, Tom is only telling his version of the truth. Amanda is still attractive and magnetic, as she demonstrates when she charms Jim in Scene 6.

So what is the real significance of Tom's words? As he struggles to exercise his new pitiless persona – the persona that will help him escape – the protagonist has to learn to push aside those he loves. The playwright reinforces this point at the end of the scene. When the yelling is over, Tom struggles into his coat, knocking over and damaging Laura's glass collection. This clumsy movement may be an accident, but the outcome of the play is clearly foreshadowed. Both women are going to be badly hurt by the young man they love so dearly. Amanda's and Laura's helplessness is conveyed when they look on aghast and motionless as Tom leaves. As he breaks out of his straitjacket, his family goes still.

However, even if he behaves and talks like a brute in the making, Tom is really a sentimentalist. He is immediately repentant when he shatters Laura's figurines. Instead of stomping off without a backward glance, Tom stares at his sister stupidly and drops awkwardly on to his knees to collect the fallen glass. He is so ashamed he cannot speak. In Scene 4 Tom will argue that man is 'by instinct a lover, a hunter, a fighter' (p. 260). Surely this attitude about human nature – poached from D. H. Lawrence – coupled with his dreams of a sensational alter ego named 'El Diablo', prove that the protagonist is a romantic dreamer? If we are in any doubt about this point, we only have to consider the screen image that is associated with Tom Wingfield throughout the play: a sailing vessel with a Jolly Roger. For all the harsh words he utters in this scene, for all the truth and lies he tells, Tom will never quite convince us that he is fundamentally different from the rest of his family. He finds reality as awkward as they do. This is why the image that best represents him is a story-book pirate ship, rather than a functional navy frigate.

In this scene it becomes clear that different types of truth are paralysing Tom. He is trapped by the inanity of his job, his mother's sententiousness and his guilty affection for his sister. The warehouse is hateful, but the alternative – leaving his mother and sister unsupported – is painful. Tom is not quite ready to act on his growing acceptance that he has to be cruel in order to keep his dream of being true to his poetic self alive. Until he has overcome the sentimentality he displays at the end of Scene 3, Tom will continue to be trapped, his only refuge his imagination. His long speech here prepares us for his aria about Malvolio the Magician in Scene 4, in which Tom begins to sound as if he is seriously planning his escape from the '2 by 4 situation' that hems him in (p. 255). In Scene 3 Tom is still at the stage of wild threats: 'Why, listen, if self is what I thought of, Mother, I'd be where he is – GONE!'. The hypothetical 'if' will become a purposeful question: 'You know it don't take much to get yourself into a nailed-up coffin, Laura. But who in hell ever got himself out of one without removing one nail?' (Scene 4, p. 255).

Tom's facility with words in Scene 3 makes him a close cousin of Malvolio, who serves as a role model. Both are capable of leaving an audience speechless – one with words, the other with the help of props. Both require practice to perfect their stunts. And both are deceivers. Malvolio's tricks are innocent, but Tom proves here that he is capable of malevolence. The cruel words of Scene 3 become deeds when Tom uses the light bill money to join the Seaman's Union. Because he has the final word in the argument that occurs here, we know that Tom will move on. His clumsy exit at the end of Scene 3 is a trial run for the permanent leave-taking that will occur when he is fired. Significantly, Tom shatters glass – a **symbol** of his sister – at the end of both this scene and Scene 7. Williams makes it clear that Tom will not be able to leave his sister behind, even when he does go.

TEXT 2 (SCENE 6, PAGES 276–77)

Amanda recalls the spring when she met Mr Wingfield

[LEGEND ON SCREEN: 'THIS IS MY SISTER: CELEBRATE HER WITH STRINGS!' MUSIC.]

AMANDA [*laughing, off*]

I'm going to show you something. I'm going to make a spectacular appearance!

LAURA

What is it, Mother?

AMANDA

Possess your soul in patience – you will see! Something I've resurrected from that old trunk! Styles haven't changed so terribly much after all. ...

[*She parts the portières.*]

Now just look at your mother!

[*She wears a girlish frock of yellowed voile with a blue silk sash. She carries a bunch of jonquils – the legend of her youth is nearly revived.*]

[*Feverishly*] This is the dress in which I led the cotillion, won the cakewalk twice at Sunset Hill, wore one spring to the Governor's ball in Jackson! See how I sashayed around the ballroom, Laura?

[*She raises her skirt and does a mincing step around the room.*]

I wore it on Sundays for my gentlemen callers! I had it on the day I met your father –

I had malaria fever all that spring. The change of climate from East Tennessee to the Delta – weakened resistance – I had a little temperature all the time – not enough to be serious – just enough to make me restless and giddy! – Invitations poured in – parties all over the Delta! – 'Stay in bed,' said mother, 'you have fever!' – but I just wouldn't. – I took quinine but kept on going, going! – Evenings, dances! – Afternoons, long, long rides! Picnics – lovely! – So lovely, that country in May. – All lacy with dogwood, literally flooded with jonquils! – That was the spring I had the craze for jonquils. – Jonquils became an absolute obsession. Mother said, 'Honey, there's no more room for jonquils.' And still I kept on bringing in more jonquils. Whenever, wherever I saw them, I'd say, 'Stop! Stop! I see jonquils!' I made the young men help me gather the jonquils! It was a joke, Amanda and her jonquils! Finally there were no more vases to hold them, every available space was filled with jonquils. No vases to hold them? All right, I'll hold them myself! And then I – [*She stops in front of the picture.* MUSIC.] met your father! Malaria fever and jonquils and then – this – boy. …

[*She switches on the rose-coloured lamp.*]

I hope they get here before it starts to rain.

[*She crosses upstage and places the jonquils in bowl on table.*]

I gave your brother a little extra change so he and Mr O'Connor could take the service car home.

LAURA [*with altered look*]
What did you say his name was?

AMANDA
O'Connor.

LAURA
What is his first name?

AMANDA
I don't remember. Oh, yes, I do. It was – Jim!

[LAURA *sways slightly and catches hold of a chair.*
LEGEND ON SCREEN: 'NOT JIM!']

LAURA [*faintly*]
Not – Jim!

AMANDA
Yes, that was it, it was Jim! I've never known a Jim that wasn't nice!

[MUSIC OMINOUS.]

LAURA

Are you sure his name is Jim O'Connor?

AMANDA

Yes. Why?

LAURA

Is he the one that Tom used to know in high school?

AMANDA

He didn't say so. I think he just got to know him at the warehouse.

LAURA

There was a Jim O'Connor we both knew in high school – [*Then, with effort.*] If that is the one that Tom is bringing to dinner – you'll have to excuse me, I won't come to the table.

This extract reveals a great deal about Amanda. We have become accustomed to her romantic style of speech, but as she prepares for the arrival of the gentleman caller, she goes further than simple reminiscence. In Scene 6 *'the legend of her youth is nearly revived'*.

Significantly, Amanda requires specific clothes to help her step back in time. She also needs a stage to burst on to. Williams has her part the portières, as if she were drawing aside curtains framing a proscenium arch. Actress that she is, Amanda enjoys dressing up for her roles. As respectable member of the DAR she sported a *'cheap or imitation velvety-looking cloth'* coat with an imitation fur collar and a hat (Scene 2, p. 241). As vulnerable, devoted mother she wore a bathrobe and curlers. Now she drags out a yellowed voile dress, **symbol** of her youthful success as Southern belle. This garment has a good deal of history attached to it. It is associated with dancing and flirting: 'See how I sashayed around the ballroom, Laura?' Amanda cries, raising her skirt and mincing across the stage. Amanda's brief recreation of the Governor's ball in Jackson suggests that the little woman has temporarily lost sight of the purpose of the evening: to find Laura a mate. This is **ironic**, since the girl has only just finished dressing herself, and the screen legend which appeared immediately before Amanda's spectacular appearance reminded us to celebrate Laura, not her mother. By saving her dramatic entrance until after her daughter has put on the costume that is intended to turn her into a pretty trap, Amanda is unconsciously stealing the limelight. This is something she will be unable to resist doing again when Jim O'Connor arrives.

The audience will feel uncomfortable watching a middle-aged woman cavorting in an old-fashioned girl's ensemble. Surely Amanda's appearance makes her ridiculous? However, she does not remain an object of amusement for long. Williams hints that Amanda is also a small-scale tragic heroine. Her obvious enjoyment of a dress that can be seen as a **symbol** of marital misery, encourages the audience to see the **pathos** of Amanda's situation. Like previous arias about Blue Mountain, the account of the spring when Mr Wingfield proposed contains a number of bad omens. To begin with, Amanda was sick with malaria when she first met her future husband. Her resistance was weakened and she was restless and giddy. The drug quinine enabled Amanda to keep on 'going, going!' with her frenetic socialising. What kind of judgements could she be expected to make in this unhealthy state?

It is not as if the young Amanda was particularly responsible or sensible when she was well. Indulged by a mother who did not have the power to make her stay in bed during a serious illness, she was driven by a frivolous desire to be seen at parties and entertain as many men as possible. The language Amanda uses to describe her fondness for jonquils indicates that she was spinning out of control: 'That was the spring I had the craze for jonquils – Jonquils became an absolute obsession.' A girl governed by crazes and obsessions is unlikely to make rational decisions about marriage. Adult Amanda is mistaken when she says, 'It was a joke, Amanda and her jonquils!' The flowers are anything but amusing. They clearly became part of the routine of drawing young men into the web: 'I made the young men help me gather the jonquils!' Eventually her bouquets overwhelmed the house completely and every available space was filled. Into this distracted house of excess stepped 'this – boy ...' who would break Amanda's heart. The fact that all the vases were full hints that Amanda should not have given the handsome Wingfield house room.

We know that Amanda made a grave mistake because her speech trails off. She is unable to continue talking about the man she loved. However, Williams reminds us that Amanda's method of dealing with the truth is to evade it. Immediately after her aria, the mother turns on the rose-coloured lamp, symbol of her romantic nature. It is sadly ironic that the lamp has been bought to help in the seduction of Jim O'Connor, and that it should be switched on after Amanda has recounted a tale of disease and poor judgement. We will not feel at all encouraged for Laura. Her mother's story acts as a guarantee that things can only turn out badly. The romantic glow of a lamp cannot save the Wingfield women. Amanda's pensive comment about the rain seems to confirm this. The bowl of jonquils placed on the table is an unhappy and ominous sight. History is repeating itself, and the consequences will again be disastrous.

Our unease about Laura has been growing steadily. While her foolish mother darts about comfortably in her resurrected dress, the girl struggles to get used to her own altered appearance as 'pretty trap'. By showing us the rituals the women go through as they put on their costumes and prepare the apartment for the gentleman caller, Williams is drawing our attention to the artificiality of the match-making scheme. Amanda may be capable of acting the part of hostess, but her daughter is not up to the role she has been cast in. Laura is unhappy about deception and pretence, as her panic about the 'Gay Deceivers' demonstrated. This girl does not have the social skills needed to conceal her shyness. We are reminded of this during the tense exchange that occurs at the end of the extract when Laura realises that the gentleman caller invited for supper is the boy she worshipped in high school. The playwright emphasises Laura's horror through the staging and dialogue. The girl is literally thrown off balance when she hears Jim's name; she *sways slightly and catches hold of a chair*, while the panic-stricken exclamation 'NOT JIM!' is projected on a screen. These words are echoed faintly when the girl speaks. The music takes on an ominous tone as Laura begins to panic. Her questions are earnest and urgent: 'Are you sure his name is Jim O'Connor?', 'Is he the one that Tom used to know in high school?'.

Up to this point in Scene 6 it is tempting to see Laura as the weak victim of her mother's machinations. She has been dressed, chided and bullied by Amanda. But the girl possesses some of the willpower that carried her mother through her jonquil-filled spring in Blue Mountain. It takes effort, but Laura is firm when she says, 'I won't come to table.' This brave statement shows that the girl is trying to gather her resources. She will need all the strength she can muster if she is to survive the evening ahead. At the end of this extract the audience will be pessimistic about the outcome for Laura. There is little hope that Amanda will begin to support her disconcerted child. The mother is too captivated by the legend of her own youth, and the need to recreate her own courtship, to pay serious attention to her daughter's emotional needs. She fails to pick up on the girl's agony when she provides cheerful, distracted answers to the queries put to her: 'I don't remember …', 'I've never known a Jim that wasn't nice!'. Not until the closing moments of Scene 6 will Amanda really see Laura clearly, at which point her dismay will mirror her daughter's. All the signs in this scene suggest that mother and daughter will share the same fate: they will both be let down by the 'deceptive rainbow', love.

TEXT 3   (SCENE 7, PAGES 302–5)

Jim and Laura dance together, bumping into the table and breaking the glass unicorn

JIM

    Ha-ha!

LAURA

    Oh, my goodness!

JIM

    Ha-ha-ha! [*They suddenly bump into the table,* JIM *stops.*] What did we hit on?

LAURA

    Table.

JIM

    Did something fall off it? I think –

LAURA

    Yes.

JIM

    I hope that it wasn't the little glass horse with the horn!

LAURA

    Yes.

JIM

    Aw, aw, aw. It is broken?

LAURA

    Now it is just like all the other horses.

JIM

    It's lost its –

LAURA

    Horn!

    It doesn't matter. Maybe it's a blessing in disguise.

JIM

You'll never forgive me. I bet that that was your favourite piece of glass.

LAURA

I don't have favourites much. It's no tragedy, Freckles. Glass breaks so easily. No matter how careful you are. The traffic jars the shelves and things fall off them.

JIM

Still I'm awfully sorry that I was the cause.

LAURA [*smiling*]

I'll just imagine he had an operation.

The horn was removed to make him feel less – freakish!

[*They both laugh.*]

Now he will feel more at home with the other horses, the ones that don't have horns. …

JIM

Ha-ha, that's very funny!

[*Suddenly serious.*]

I'm glad to see that you have a sense of humour.

You know – you're – well – very different!

Surprisingly different from anyone else I know!

[*His voice becomes soft and hesitant with a genuine feeling.*]

Do you mind me telling you that?

[LAURA *is abashed beyond speech.*]

I mean it in a nice way …

[LAURA *nods shyly, looking away.*]

You make me feel sort of – I don't know how to put it!

I'm usually pretty good at expressing things, but –

This is something that I don't know how to say!

[LAURA *touches her throat and clears it – turns the broken unicorn in her hands. Even softer.*]

Has anyone ever told you that you were pretty?

[PAUSE: MUSIC.

   LAURA *looks up slowly, with wonder, and shakes her head.*]

Well, you are! In a very dfferent way from anyone else. And all the nicer because of the difference, too.

[*His voice becomes low and husky.* LAURA *turns away, nearly faint with the novelty of her emotions.*]

I wish that you were my sister. I'd teach you to have some confidence in yourself. The different people are not like other people, but being different is nothing to be ashamed of. Because other people are not such wonderful people. They're one hundred times one thousand. You're one times one! They walk all over the earth. You just stay here. They're common as – weeds, but – you – well, you're – *Blue Roses*!

[IMAGE ON SCREEN: BLUE ROSES.

   MUSIC CHANGES.]

LAURA

But blue is wrong for – roses …

JIM

It's right for you! – You're – pretty!

LAURA

In what respect am I pretty?

JIM

In all respects – believe me! Your eyes – your hair – are pretty! Your hands are pretty!

[*He catches hold of her hand.*]

You think I'm making this up because I'm invited to dinner and have to be nice. Oh, I could do that! I could put on an act for you, Laura, and say lots of things without being very sincere. But this time I am. I'm talking to you sincerely. I happened to notice you had this inferiority complex that keeps you from feeling comfortable with people. Somebody needs to build your confidence up and make you proud instead of shy and turning away and – blushing – Somebody – ought to – Ought to – *kiss* you, Laura!

For many, this is the most moving and significant episode in *The Glass Menagerie*. Laura and Jim bring the best out of each other, achieving a fleeting but real intimacy in the aftermath of their clumsy waltz. Unfortunately, we know that the mutual regard they enjoy for a few moments cannot last because Laura's favourite treasure is broken.

Jim has been full of good intentions throughout Scene 7. He urges Laura to dance because he wants her to break through her inferiority complex and let herself go in an unselfconscious way. Laura was convinced that her companion would not be able to 'budge' her, that she would step on and hurt him. But Jim proved that she was wrong. The waltz made them both happy. Jim's laughter, 'Ha-ha-ha!' and Laura's exclamation, 'Oh, my goodness!' confirm their enjoyment. Because she is more relaxed than we have seen her at any other time in the play – except when she was alone with her menagerie at the beginning of Scene 2 – Laura is able to take the destruction of her unicorn in her stride. She even says that it might be 'a blessing in disguise', a comment which suggests she is glad to have been offered the opportunity to behave like an ordinary young woman, and leave her solitary world behind. Laura clearly values the connection she has been able to make with Jim; she fondly calls him 'Freckles' and pretends that she doesn't have a favourite glass animal, contradicting a statement she made earlier in the scene. The girl works hard to put Jim at his ease after the accident, just as he has worked hard to draw her out. There is more shared laughter as Laura smiles and says she will 'just imagine he had an operation …', 'Now he will feel more at home with the other horses, the ones that don't have horns …'. Our hearts will go out to Laura here. The generosity of this timid girl shows how deeply she has been touched by the gentleman caller.

Jim is also deeply touched by his fragile companion, whose awkwardness he mirrors when he exclaims, 'This is something that I don't know how to say!' It becomes clear that he appreciates Laura's kindness because he suddenly becomes serious and speaks softly and hesitantly with genuine feeling. Jim's compliments show that he recognises Laura's gentle loveliness. He admires her sense of humour – which we know he is responsible for unlocking – and the prettiness of her eyes, hair and hands. Some of what he says may seem like conventional praise, but when Jim reminds her of her nickname, 'Blue Roses', he is celebrating Laura's difference and trying to boost her confidence by reassuring her that it is a good thing to be unique, or as he puts it, 'one times one'. To his credit, Jim also looks beyond Laura's appearance. When he catches hold of the girl's hand he delivers a speech which reconfirms his understanding of Laura's shyness.

It is at this point that things begin to go wrong. Jim is more robust than Laura. His voice may be low and husky, but the young man's eloquence is proof of his self-command. During his flattering portrait of her, Laura is close to fainting. The stage directions remind us of her fragility. She is '*abashed beyond speech*', she reaches to touch her throat and clears it but remains silent, she '*looks up slowly, with wonder, and shakes her head*', turning away when she is asked if she has ever been told she is pretty. We know that the novelty of her emotions is dangerous. If the girl reacts so strongly to kind words, how will she cope if she is touched? Like her unicorn, which was broken when it was knocked off the table, Laura will suffer badly when she receives a physical jolt. Sadly, in spite of the delight she takes in being lured out of her frozen, private world, the girl is simply not hardy enough to thrive elsewhere. We know that Jim's kiss has the power to wound as well as heal her.

The staging, **symbolism** and **imagery** suggest that permanent healing is not really a possibility. Laura clings to the unicorn throughout this exchange, giving the lie to her comment that the accident isn't a tragedy. In fact, the breakage matters a great deal. A unicorn without a horn is not really like other horses; it is damaged, and 'freakish' and will not 'feel at home'. Like the trucks that have previously rumbled past the apartment, causing havoc in the menagerie, Jim will destroy Laura's universe. The screen image of blue roses reminds us that Laura is a vulnerable hothouse flower who cannot survive among the common weeds, which Jim says 'walk all over the earth'.

Seemingly innocent remarks made by Jim and Laura reinforce these points and confirm the fact that the couple are fundamentally incompatible, and that the intimacy achieved will be destroyed. When the unicorn is knocked off the table, Jim refers to the figurine as 'the little glass horse with the horn'. Why does he not remember its special name? Laura is correct when she says 'blue is wrong for – roses…' Blue roses do not exist in the real world. So Jim's insistence that the nickname is 'right for you' is a backhanded compliment. In addition, the audience will remember that Laura's nickname was arrived at as the result of a misunderstanding. Are other blunders therefore inevitable? Laura's first important conversation with Jim at high school occurred as a result of illness. In Scene 6 we learned that Amanda's attraction to Mr Wingfield began when she was feverish with malaria. By linking the two female characters and their beaux through disease, Williams makes it plain that Laura will suffer for loving Jim, just as her mother was reduced to misery by her husband.

Finally, the topics discussed in this extract suggest that the intimacy established is constantly under threat. A discussion about a girl's fantasy world of glass consolidates a connection forged by a brief turn around the room. When he praises Laura, the gentleman caller is responding to a beauty which the playwright insists is 'momentary ... not actual, not lasting' (Scene 6, p. 274). Furthermore, Jim remains preoccupied with amateur psychology and his own notions about dealing with an inferiority complex. At times the gentleman caller is seduced by the sound of his own voice, and loses sight of Laura. If he thought more carefully about the effect of his words, he might not make the error of physically approaching 'Blue Roses'. But perhaps this impetuosity is to be expected. Jim enjoyed being 'beleaguered by females' (Scene 7, p. 296) at high school, and the silent admiration he can undoubtedly see in Laura's face and coy gestures would spur most men on. Equally, if Laura was stronger she would be able to speak and break into Jim's reverie, perhaps preventing the fatal kiss. But we can understand her weakness. Jim talks like a lover. He flatters Laura's looks and makes remarks designed to win any girl's heart: 'I could put on an act for you' and 'I'm talking to you sincerely'. In the circumstances, Laura can be forgiven for overlooking Jim's comment about wishing she were his sister. The audience, however, will recognise that Jim's wish is the signal that Laura's dreams will be shattered.

PART FIVE

BACKGROUND

WILLIAMS' LIFE AND WORKS

Thomas Lanier Williams was born on 26 March 1911 in Columbus, Mississippi. He adopted the name Tennessee in 1939. Sometimes he claimed that this was a nickname given to him by classmates, who could only remember that he was from 'a southern state with a long name. And when they couldn't think of Mississippi, they settled on Tennessee. That was all right with me, so when it stuck I changed it permanently'. On other occasions Williams said that he chose the name because some of his family had fought the Indians for Tennessee, and that 'the defense of a stockade against a band of savages was consistent with a writer's hard life' (Donald Spoto, *The Kindness of Strangers, The Life of Tennessee Williams*, p. 67) However he came by his name, it certainly suited the content, style and tone of his dramatic works, which were influenced and inspired by his family history and early childhood in the American South.

Williams' father, Cornelius Coffin Williams, a travelling salesman for a telephone company, who briefly studied law and fought in the Spanish-American war, married his mother, Edwina Dakin, the daughter of an Episcopalian minister, in 1907. The union was not a great success and within a year Edwina had returned to her family, pregnant with her first child, Rose, who was born in 1909. It was not until 1918, when Cornelius was promoted to a managerial position in the International Shoe Company in St Louis, Missouri, that the family were permanently reunited under one roof. The portrait painted of the absent father 'who fell in love with long distance' and the melodramatic, talkative Southern belle who looks back with longing at her exuberant, genteel youth in *The Glass Menagerie* offers the reader a glimpse of the Williams' marriage as seen through their son's eyes.

The move to St Louis, where *The Glass Menagerie* is set, was a traumatic one for Tom and his sister Rose. The children had grown up comfortably and peacefully in the bosom of their mother's family in the Clarksdale rectory, where they had become accustomed to a certain amount of prestige due to their grandfather's position as a minister. Life in the

South had been gracious and leisurely; in the Midwestern city of St Louis Tom and Rose were mocked for their accents and manners and forced to adapt to a more hectic, urban environment. They found themselves first in a boarding house and then in a series of depressing apartments. The children were frightened of their father, whom they had previously known only as a visitor. He seemed only to care for his second son, Dakin (born in 1919), dismissing Tom as 'Miss Nancy' because he felt 'an excessive attachment to the female members of my family' and preferred reading, writing and movie-going to baseball. Cornelius was an overbearing and at times quarrelsome man, who took to drink, womanising and gambling as his marriage deteriorated. He kept his family short of money in spite of earning a good wage. For her part, the impractical Edwina found it very difficult to adapt to life as a city housewife. Cooking and domestic chores were not her forte, and she resented the life to which her irresponsible husband seemed to have reduced her. As a result of their difficult circumstances, Tom and Rose, who were always close as children, became even more heavily reliant on one another for emotional support and companionship.

By the late 1920s life in the Williams household had become in Dakin's words, 'just terrible'. Edwina had been ill a number of times and Rose's increasing mental instability was a serious cause for concern. After a very welcome respite in the form of a trip to Europe with some of his grandfather's parishioners in 1928, Tom graduated from high school in June 1929. He was considered an average student, but he had had some success writing poems, reviews and articles, which were published in school magazines. Already he had begun to see writing as a 'refuge' from 'the world of reality in which I felt acutely uncomfortable'. Because of his grandparents' financial generosity Tom was able to enter the University of Missouri at Columbia, where he studied liberal arts. Absent minded and shy, he failed to shine academically. When he received poor grades in the summer of 1931 his father insisted that Tom be put to work as an office clerk at the International Shoe Company for three months. Tom loathed this job, describing his time at the shoe company as 'a living death'. He did not give up on his literary ambitions, however, and, like his namesake in *The Glass Menagerie*, worked late into the night on his short stories and poems. In 1959 he said 'I've always been blocked as a writer but my desire to write has been so strong that it has always broken down the block and gone past it' (*New York Times*, 8 March, 1959).

performed in 1947. *Streetcar* tells the story of a faded and damaged
Southern belle, Blanche DuBois, who bears a number of resemblances to
both Amanda and Laura (and, it has been said, to both Rose and
Tennessee Williams.) Blanche mourns the passing of the old, genteel ways
of the South and is haunted by the memory of the suicide of her young
homosexual husband, Allan. She finds it impossible to negotiate the harsh
reality of life in the cramped New Orleans home of her sister Stella and
brash brother-in-law Stanley. Having lost her home, her relatives and her
job, Blanche finally loses her sanity when she is raped by Stanley. At the
end of the play she is led away to an institution by a doctor.

The success of *Streetcar*, a Pulitzer Prize winner, made Williams a
wealthy man. From this point onwards there was a Tennessee Williams
play in production on Broadway almost every other year for over a decade.
Williams' travels also began to follow a pattern. He would spend time in
Europe, periodically returning to New Orleans, Key West, New York and
other American locations. His most important plays of this period
(1947–61) include *Summer and Smoke* (1948), *The Rose Tattoo* (1951),
Camino Real (1953), *Cat on a Hot Tin Roof* (1955), *Orpheus Descending*
(1957), which was a remake of an earlier play, *Battle of Angels*, *Suddenly
Last Summer* (1958), *Sweet Bird of Youth* (1959) and *The Night of The
Iguana* (1961), which was Williams' last great stage success.

For *Cat* Williams received a second Pulitzer Prize. Like all his dramatic
works, the play contains a portrait of an unforgettable female character.
Maggie the Cat is a tenacious young woman, frustrated by her husband
Brick, a former high-school athlete who is sinking into alcoholism after the
death of his friend Skipper. Determined that her brother and sister-in-law
and their tribe of 'no-neck monsters' should not inherit the family fortune
when Brick's father, Big Daddy, succumbs to cancer, Maggie struggles to
hold her fragile marriage together. The play is an examination of greed,
envy and crippling self-deception, a theme which preoccupies Williams
again in *Suddenly Last Summer*. A long one-act play in four scenes, *Suddenly*
tells the disturbing tale of an unpleasant and manipulative young man,
Sebastian Venable. Because of a stroke, his mother Violet has not been able
to travel abroad with her son, so he is accompanied by his young cousin
Catharine, who recounts Sebastian's horrible death at the hands of a group
of young boys to whom he made homosexual advances. Unable to accept
her niece's version of events, Violet has had Catharine incarcerated in a

mental asylum and engaged a neurosurgeon to perform a lobotomy on her. At the end of the play the doctor realises that Catharine's story is true and confronts Violet.

In *Sweet Bird of Youth*, which Williams described as 'an examination of what is really corrupt in life', we witness the disintegration of a fading movie actress, Alexandra Del Lago, known as 'Princess', who attempts to assuage her feelings of emptiness by turning to drugs, alcohol and young lovers. *The Night of the Iguana* started life as a short story of the same name. It became an evocative and poetic drama which explores ideas about art, religion and the poet's vocation. It contains a cast of intriguing, fragile characters who have all ended up on the coast of Mexico: a tormented, alcoholic, defrocked priest 'at the end of his rope', the Reverend T. Lawrence Shannon; a shy, artistic spinster, Hannah Jelkes, and her poet grandfather, Jonathan Coffin. The hotel where these characters stay is presided over by a crude, middle aged woman, Maxine Faulk, whose loquacity recalls Amanda from *The Glass Menagerie*. The play closes more optimistically than many of Williams' other dramas, with Shannon accepting the possibility of a new life with Maxine.

Critics have suggested that Williams' oeuvre became more uneven after the triumph of *Cat on a Hot Tin Roof*. It is certainly true that the plays he wrote after *The Night of the Iguana* failed to capture the critics' admiration in the way that his work of the 1940s and early 1950s had done. During the late 1950s and 1960s, Williams suffered a number of personal crises and traumas, which seemed to drain him emotionally and creatively. In 1963 his long-term lover, Frank Merlo, died of cancer. This event profoundly affected the playwright and he became seriously depressed. Williams was also terrified of going mad, and became a hypochondriac, convinced that every play he wrote would be his last because he was dying. Like Alexandra Del Lago in *Sweet Bird of Youth*, he sought refuge in drugs, alcohol and affairs. He also attempted to try to come to terms with some of the issues that troubled him through psychoanalysis. After *Iguana*, his best known work of the 1960s is probably *The Milktrain Doesn't Stop Here Any More* (1963).

In the 1970s Williams continued to write productively, and although critics were no longer responding so enthusiastically to his work, there were productions of *Small Craft Warnings* (1972), *Outcry* (1973), *Vieux Carre* (1979) and *A Lovely Sunday for Creve Coeur* (1980). The last original

Williams play to be produced on Broadway was *Clothes for a Summer Hotel* (1980). It received bad notices and closed quickly. Theatres outside New York continued to put on the playwright's subsequent dramas, and his reputation abroad grew as Williams' work was translated into other languages. Williams continued to write short stories, novels and poetry throughout the final decades of his life, also publishing his highly readable and revealing, though not consistently reliable, *Memoirs* in 1975. By the time of his death in February 1983 – he choked to death on the cap of a bottle of barbiturates – Tennessee Williams was established as one of the most pre-eminent American dramatists of the twentieth century.

Fifteen films have been made based on Williams' work. He collaborated on seven of them and also wrote screenplays, including *Baby Doll* (1951). Williams' feelings about the screen versions of his work were at best ambivalent, although he was reasonably content with the results of the film version of his best novel, *The Roman Spring of Mrs Stone* (1961).

LITERARY BACKGROUND

SOUTHERN LITERATURE

Until the 1920s the South was culturally and intellectually overshadowed by the rest of the United States. This is not to say that the South did not possess its own distinctive literary traditions. After the American Civil War (1861–65), when the Southern Confederate Army was defeated, writers began to mythologise the South and its characteristic ways of life. These tales featured 'pure women and splendid gentlemen', who lived out their lives in sumptuous mansions (Ursula Brumm, 'William Faulkner and the Southern Renaissance', *American Literature Since 1900*, ed. Marcus Cunliffe, Penguin, 1993, p. 175). This vein of romanticism continued to thrive in the early part of the twentieth century. In 1936 Margaret Mitchell had a runaway success with *Gone With the Wind*, which won the Pulitzer Prize, and was made into an immensely popular film.

Southern authors had always been imaginative, and by the 1930s new writers, with very different ideas, had begun to make names for themselves. The sentimental myths about the Old South began to be transformed. The renaissance was led by William Faulkner (1897–1962), whose works move beyond simple nostalgia to critical reassessment of the past. Greed, violence, dishonesty and decadence dominate Faulkner's novels, which are as much concerned with moral decay as with bravery and endurance. The families he writes about are stained by the sins of the past, in particular, the Southern sin of slavery. Faulkner's most important novels of the 1920s and 1930s are *The Sound and the Fury* (1929), *As I Lay Dying* (1930), *Light in August* (1932) and *Absalom, Absalom!* (1936).

AMERICAN DRAMA PRE-1940

Eugene O'Neill (1883–1953) is considered by many to be the first really important American dramatist of the twentieth century. He remained a dominant figure throughout his lifetime, and is the author of several plays which have proved to possess enduring merits, including *Anna Christie* (1921), *The Hairy Ape* (1922), *Strange Interlude* (1928), *Mourning Becomes Electra* (first performed 1931) and two later masterpieces, *The Iceman Cometh* (written 1939, first performed 1946) and *Long Day's Journey Into Night* (written 1940, first performed 1956). In the 1920s O'Neill went through an **expressionist** phase, which marked him out from the other dramatists of the time, who were predominantly **naturalists**. Like Williams, O'Neill was interested in creating characters who were psychologically credible. In his work he focused on tension-ridden and dysfunctional families and individuals, who were striving to understand themselves and their connections with the rest of mankind. O'Neill's characters are often deluded, or living in the grips of their illusions.

During the first decades of the twentieth century the dominant genre was **melodrama**. Acting styles and production methods were, however, predominantly naturalistic. By the 1920s, and then later, as the Depression tightened its grip on the nation, the drama of social concern became more popular with audiences. Some of these plays have been dismissed as sentimental, but a number of the so-called propaganda plays of the 1930s remain powerful. Two plays written by Clifford Odets (1906–63) stand out: *Waiting for Lefty* (1935), about a taxi drivers' strike, and *Awake And Sing* (1935), which focuses on the disappointments suffered by a Jewish family. The work of Maxwell Anderson (1888–1959), Thornton Wilder (1897–1975) and Lillian Hellman (born 1905) also deserve consideration. Anderson was attracted to writing in a poetic style about individuals who prefer to accept defeat heroically. His verse play *Winterset* (1935) was based on a notorious real-life murder case which provoked an outcry against the injustices of the American legal system. Wilder's work is more optimistic in tone than that of many of his contemporaries, although he, too, was concerned about the real hardships that people faced during the Depression. Wilder had a great success with *Our Town* (1938), which features a sympathetic narrator who introduces and frames events. Lillian Hellman wrote traditional well-made plays, but her themes were often controversial, and the mood she creates is dark. In *The Children's Hour* (1934) two schoolteacher sisters are accused of lesbianism. In *Days to Come* (1936) gangsters are brought in to break up a strike in a factory and a striker is framed for a murder. *The Little Foxes* (1939) tells the story of the unscrupulous Hubbard family, whose personal and business dealings are equally cruel and exploitative.

Williams swept on to the theatrical scene like a breath of spring wind, as did his contemporary Arthur Miller (born 1915). Both were considered worthy inheritors of O'Neill's crown. Williams learned from O'Neill's **modernist** techniques, particularly his use of **symbolism**, while Miller echoed the earlier dramatist's interest in exploring the individual's responsibilities to himself and society in *All My Sons* (1947) and *Death of a Salesman* (1949). In their early dramas, which deal with the delusions and frustrations bred by the American dream, Williams and Miller captured the mood of doubt and bewilderment that their generation felt in the post-war years.

Williams' influences

Unsurprisingly, given his own personal experiences growing up with a backward-looking mother in a delightful home in Mississippi, Williams was attracted to a number of the myths about the South. His adolescent loathing of St Louis confirmed his suspicion of the North, and its industrialised and materialistic ways. But, like Faulkner, he was able to see the faults and absurdities of the Old South, as well as its charms.

When he began writing drama, Williams turned to European models for inspiration. As a young man he studied the works of Henrik Ibsen, August Strindberg and Anton Chekhov, who particularly appealed to him. The mixture of **irony**, **pathos** and comedy that characterises *The Glass Menagerie* has been labelled Chekhovian. Like Chekhov, Williams writes sympathetically about people who are deceived by their illusions and rejects the neat closure of the clear, simple, happy ending. The psycho-logical realism for which these European dramatists have been praised is also something that Williams was keen to achieve.

Williams was a poet as well as a dramatist. He discovered the Romantic poetry of Byron, Keats and Shelley early on, and also admired the work of the French neo-romantic symbolists, Proust, Baudelaire and Rimbaud. But the poet who perhaps had the greatest influence on him was the American, Hart Crane (1899–1932). Williams identified strongly with Crane, whose life-story bore a startling resemblance to his own. Crane grew up in an unhappy home in Ohio, where he was coddled by an overbearing mother and a constant source of disappointment to his difficult father. Like Williams, Crane rejected his father's values and set out to become a poet. He believed that the life of the artist was one of necessity, and that in order to be true to his calling, the poet must accept isolation and guilt uncom-plainingly. These ideas perhaps informed Williams' conception of his poet-narrator Tom. The war between the spirit and the flesh preoccupied Crane, as it would perplex Williams, who would also, like his hero, become dependent on alcohol. There was another important reason why Williams felt that Crane was 'a brother under the skin': he was a promiscuous homosexual with self-destructive tendencies.

SOURCES

Williams often recycled his work. *The Glass Menagerie* is a successful reworking of three previous attempts at telling Rose Williams' story; a sixteen-page short story, 'Portrait of a Girl in Glass', which was probably written in 1941–42, an unpublished one-act play in five scenes, *If You Breathe it Breaks*, which Williams wrote before he started work in Hollywood in 1943, and a film scenario rejected by MGM, entitled *The Gentleman Caller*. 'Portrait of a Girl in Glass' tells the tale of a naive, simple-minded and rather odd girl, and her mother and brother. A gentleman caller arrives, but Laura is not perturbed by his presence and does not fall apart when he reveals he is going steady with another girl. Tom's closing narrative in *The Glass Menagerie* is almost lifted wholesale from this short story. *If You Breathe It Breaks* focuses on a girl who loves her glass collection. There are two brothers, and a mother who is determined to procure a gentleman caller to woo her daughter. In this play the girl rejects the caller, commenting that while she does not mind watching boys go past the house while she sits on the porch, she has no desire to meet them. Williams expanded the scenario he wrote for MGM when it was rejected, and in each successive script the theme of escape became more prominent. He adds to the **pathos** of his successful drama by making Laura shy and withdrawn, but not simple-minded, as she is in the short story. Perhaps the playwright believed that it is easier to identify with a heroine who suffers because she is timid, rather than mentally deficient in an unspecified way. Empathy is also increased because Laura genuinely cares for Jim in *The Glass Menagerie* – he is a real loss. Her counterpart in *If You Breathe It Breaks* is perhaps too detached from love to invite sympathy.

The personal experiences that Williams drew on when composing *The Glass Menagerie* are well documented. Critics have suggested that the glass-loving girl in the one-act play is replaced by a more complex young woman, whose history and interests reflect those of both Rose and Tennessee Williams. Rose loved her victrola records as much as Laura, and she attended the Rubicam Business College, which proved as uncongenial in real life as it is in *The Glass Menagerie*. The campaign to find her a husband did not begin until four years after her college failure, however. In her early twenties, Rose was, in fact, a popular young woman, who was not short of callers. Although a young man called Jim Connor did call on Rose, he was not a real love, but a casual college acquaintance of Tom's. As a child and adolescent, Tom was far more shy and reticent than his sister, who was chatty and often outgoing, though as her mental health deteriorated, she became increasingly agitated and loquacious. It was only after her lobotomy that Rose Williams withdrew, becoming a pale imitation of her former self. The reader may wonder why Tennessee Williams makes Laura sad rather than unstable; is it because he wished to preserve his sister's dignity? Williams dealt with the subject of madness in a number of plays he wrote after *The Glass Menagerie*, most notably in *A Streetcar Named Desire*.

The real-life story and legend that surround Laura's glass menagerie is amusing. According to Williams' younger brother Dakin, Rose was not an avid collector of figurines, although she owned a few cheap glass items. The real collection belonged to a Mrs Maggie Wingfield, whose name Williams borrowed. She was a resident of Clarksdale, Mississippi, where Tom and Rose lived with their mother's family, before they moved to St Louis. She displayed her glass collection in her front window. Later, in interviews,

y

Tennessee Williams claimed that Rose had a large collection, which he helped to build up. This kind of mythologising was typical of the playwright, who often embroidered the truth to make it more poetic or apt.

Although Williams' mother apparently failed to see the likeness, Amanda Wingfield is, according to Dakin Williams, a fairly accurate portrait of Edwina. In *The Glass Menagerie* Clarksdale is transformed into Blue Mountain. On one occasion Edwina received as many as thirty gentlemen callers, a figure which puts Amanda's seventeen in the shade. Cornelius Coffin Williams did not desert his wife, although until the family moved to St Louis, he was frequently away on business. The Wingfield home is based on a small apartment the Williamses lived in when they first arrived in St Louis. Music from a nearby ballroom, which resembled the Paradise Dance Hall, could be heard from across the alley. In *The Glass Menagerie* Williams makes the father an enigmatic man who cleared off when his children were young. This enables the playwright to make Tom's predicament more desperate because his mother and sister have no one else to rely on. Tom Wingfield's movements are much more severely restricted than Tennessee Williams' were.

HISTORICAL BACKGROUND

The Glass Menagerie is set in 1937–38, during the Great Depression, on which the narrator looks back. Tom's narratives seem to be delivered in the present (the early 1940s), which would suggest he has survived the first few years of the Second World War. A third time period is mentioned – his mother's youth in the South. Amanda Wingfield would have reached adulthood and married at around the time that the First World War was being fought. Her husband, Mr Wingfield, served in this war. An understanding of the events of these periods is useful when trying to consider the dramatist's conception of the past, and the relationship it has to the present in *The Glass Menagerie*.

THE OLD SOUTH AND THE FIRST WORLD WAR (1914–18)

Historically, the Old South consisted of eleven states, which united in a confederacy to fight the rest of the country during the American Civil War (1861–65). The economy of these states was reliant on slave labour, especially the tobacco and cotton industries. The North had agitated for the abolition of slavery for a long period, which finally broke out on 12 April 1861. In 1861 the population of the South was approximately nine million people, which included three million slaves, while the North had a population of twenty-two million. Ultimately, it was no surprise when the South was defeated; the North had more men, more money and a greater manufacturing capacity.

After the Civil War the South suffered a long period of economic decline, which had a significant impact on the lifestyles of the great plantation owners. Many Southerners regretted the passing of their old culture, which was genteel, leisured, and, for the leading families, privileged. The backward-looking conservatism of the South is highlighted by Amanda's membership of the DAR in *The Glass Menagerie*. This patriotic women's organisation was originally founded in the 1890s, the period during which Amanda would have been born in Blue Mountain.

When the First World War began in August 1914, it looked as if it would not last for very long. President Woodrow Wilson was keen to adopt a neutral policy, and initially succeeded in keeping his nation out of the war. Relations between the USA and Germany deteriorated, however, after a German U-boat torpedoed a British passenger ship in May 1915. There were 128 Americans among the 1,200 people who died. Eventually, Wilson declared war on 6 April 1917. By the end of the war, there were over four million men in the US Army, almost three million of whom had been conscripted. Of the two million American troops who fought, 112,432 died.

THE GREAT DEPRESSION (1929–41)

The Wall Street Crash of 29 October 1929 spelled disaster for millions of Americans. The free-wheeling spending and speculation of the 1920s was over, and people were laid off from their jobs when stock prices plummeted. The president at the time, Herbert Hoover, tried hard to reassure the population that prosperity was just around the corner. The government relief programmes which were put in place were not sufficient to meet the demands of the desperate population. It is estimated that as many as twenty-five per cent of the workforce was jobless during the worst years of the Depression.

Throughout this period, the gangster culture that had been spawned during Prohibition (1920–33), when alcohol was made illegal, continued to flourish. The most notorious incident of gang violence was the St Valentine's Day massacre, in 1929, when Al Capone arranged the killing of a rival mobster and his associates. In *The Glass Menagerie* Tom does not speak of the Hogan gang in admiring terms, but the life of the underworld appeals to him because it is unconventional. Tom, like so many of his real-life contemporaries during the Depression, seeks respite at the movies from the crushing disappointments of everyday existence. The more conservative Jim prefers to focus on the possibility of a brighter future.

THE SECOND WORLD WAR (1939–45)

In 1934, Adolf Hitler came to power in Germany. He began a massive armaments programme, and in 1936 he sent his troops into the Rhineland. The Allies did not step in, and in 1938 the Nazi dictator invaded Austria and demanded that western Czechoslovakia be annexed by Germany, too. In 1939, when Germany invaded Poland, Britain and France finally acted. By this point, Albania had already been annexed by the Italian dictator Mussolini, who had supported Hitler when he moved into the Rhineland, and the Nazis had seized the rest of Czechoslovakia and the Polish corridor.

As was the case in the First World War, America initially stayed out of the hostilities. President Roosevelt did, however, authorise the manufacture and sale of military supplies and he negotiated an aid programme for Britain. America officially joined the Second World War after Japanese aircraft attacked Pearl Harbor on 7 December 1941. American troops served in the Far East, leading assaults against the Japanese, as well as in Europe. They participated in the decisive D-Day landings in France in June 1944. At the end of April 1945, Hitler committed suicide in a bunker in Berlin. His senior officers surrendered approximately a week later. The war in the Pacific ended when American planes dropped atom bombs on Hiroshima and Nagasaki in Japan in August 1945.

PART SIX

C RITICAL HISTORY

E ARLY RECEPTION OF *THE GLASS MENAGERIE*

The Glass Menagerie was the sixth or seventh full-length play by Tennessee Williams, and his first critical and commercial success. It transferred from Chicago to New York – where it ran for 561 performances – in 1945. Laurette Taylor, the famous American actress of the 1930s who first played Amanda, was singled out for praise by reviewers. Harold Clurman of *The Nation* said that she had 'an unforgettable fragrance and glow' which enabled her to bring out the poignancy of the character's situation. In *The New Republic* Stark Young claimed that Amanda was the best-written and most realistic character he had seen in four years. He admired Williams' 'free and true' use of language, commenting that there was 'the echo of great literature' in Amanda's Southern speech.

The *Glass Menagerie* was considered an original play because it focused on a part of the country not then well known. Later, critics would consider it in relation to the playwright's other dramas set in the South (sometimes referred to as 'Southern Gothic'), which are considered more hysterical and violent than this muted work. Interest in the ways in which Williams mythologised the Old South would continue for many years. In the 1940s, restraint was what theatre and cinema audiences were used to, and Williams' sensitive handling of his delicate characters ensured a positive reception. Audiences enjoyed the tone, which blended humour with compassion, and derision with pity, qualities which would subsequently be identified as Tennessee Williams' trademarks. One of the playwright's influences was quickly picked up on. Louis Kronenberger commented, 'in its mingled **pathos** and comedy, its mingled naturalistic detail and gauzy atmosphere, its preoccupation with memory, its tissue of forlorn hopes and backward looks and languishing self pities, *The Glass Menagerie* is more than just a little Chekhovian.' Early critics were also interested in the way in which Williams transformed his own experiences into art.

There were, however, dissenting voices. Some reviewers declared that the play was too 'wet-eyed'. Others felt that the parallels between Tom and his father should have been heightened, and that the theatrical effects the

Y

playwright called for, in particular the screen device, were distracting and unnecessary.

LATER VIEWS OF THE PLAY

When it was produced on Broadway in 1965, *The Glass Menagerie* proved that it was an enduring success. It enjoyed the longest run of any American play in revival for twenty-five years. By this point Tennessee Williams was an established playwright, and there was a large body of work with which to compare *The Glass Menagerie*. It was generally agreed that his first commercially successful play was more high-minded and tender, but less moralistic, than later dramas.

Several common approaches to Williams' oeuvre emerged. Interest in the autobiographical dimension of the playwright's work continued. Some saw *The Glass Menagerie* as a personal lament for Rose Williams and an elegy for the dramatist's own lost innocence. Psychological and moral evaluations of the characters led to sympathetic readings of Amanda in particular, while thematic approaches concentrated on the ways in which Williams presented neurotic heroines, family relationships and escapism. Williams himself said that 'all the characters in *The Glass Menagerie* try to avoid confronting unpleasant truths'. The political and religious dimensions of Williams' work have been discussed repeatedly. The playwright declared that he did not deal with social problems because they were not the problems that moved him, but early in his career he had written what might be termed protest plays, and critics now looked more closely at the social comment that appears in Tom's narratives. By the end of the twentieth century, critics were also debating Williams' portrayal of sexuality, gender and sexual politics. Women are considered to be the subjects who desire something in his work, while men are often emasculated figures. To a certain extent, this is true of *The Glass Menagerie*. Amanda is driven by a desire for love, while Jim and Tom are uncomfortable about loving. David Savran has even suggested that Tom is a closet homosexual, whose movie-going perhaps serves as a smoke-screen for other night-time activities.

Aspects of Williams' dramaturgy and the functions of his theatricalism have already been explored. One of the key controversies has been the use of slide projections in *The Glass Menagerie*. In the original Chicago production, they were abandoned, and although Williams restored them when the playtext was published, they have not always been used by acting companies. Critics nevertheless agree that Williams was breaking new ground in the 1940s, when audiences were familiar with realism, but not with expressionistic and non-naturalistic lighting, music or sets. The impression of psychological realism that Williams was aiming at in his early play was something other playwrights began to emulate. In 1984 Arthur Miller offered a posthumous tribute to his contemporary, commenting that Tennessee Williams:

> broke new ground by opening up the stage to sheer sensibility, and not by abandoning dramatic structure but transforming it. What was new in Tennessee Williams was his rhapsodic insistence on making form serve his utterance … With *The Glass Menagerie*, the long-lost lyrical line was found again, and supporting it, driving it on an emotional heroism … what he was celebrating was not approval or disapproval but humanity, the pure form of enduring life.
>
> (speech to the American Academy, 'A Memorial Tribute to Tennessee Williams')

Later critics have produced detailed studies of the parallels between Williams' work and that of other novelists, dramatists and poets. Fruitful comparisons have been drawn between Lawrence's *Sons and Lovers* and *The Glass Menagerie*. Both texts feature strong mothers, absent or weak fathers, sons who hope to forge lives for themselves as artists and delicate young women caught up in sad love affairs. *The Glass Menagerie* has been compared to Chekhov's *The Cherry Orchard* and *The Seagull*. In the former, a charming, unrealistic and backward-looking aristocrat's childhood home comes under threat when the family loses its wealth. *The Cherry Orchard* also features a young poet with radical values, who is at odds with the society he lives in. *The Seagull* focuses on four characters who all bear similarities to the cast of *The Glass Menagerie*; an aspiring writer who struggles to free himself from his family, an egotistical older woman, and a fragile girl who is attracted to a destructive outsider. Chekhov's characters are all dreamers, like the Wingfields and their gentleman caller. The influence of one of Williams' favourite poets, Hart Crane, has been noted. The title of *The Glass Menagerie* was perhaps inspired by Crane's poem, 'The Wine Menagerie', which appeared in the collection *White Buildings*. Like Williams, Crane explored the fight between the spirit and the flesh and the struggle through which the solitary poet has to go to achieve artistic integrity.

For details of the critics quoted here, see Further Reading in Broader Perspectives.

PART SEVEN

Broader perspectives

Further reading

The text

Tennessee Williams, *A Streetcar Named Desire and Other Plays*, ed. E. Martin Browne, Penguin Twentieth Century Classics, 1962
The edition of the text referred to in these Notes. Includes *Sweet Bird of Youth*, *A Streetcar Named Desire* and *The Glass Menagerie*

Tennessee Williams, *The Glass Menagerie*, Methuen, London, 2000
Includes detailed commentary and notes by Stephen J. Bottoms

Tennessee Williams, *The Glass Menagerie*, Heinemann, 1968, 1981
Introduction by E. R. Wood

Biographies

There are a number of biographies of Tennessee Williams. Two of the best are:

Ronald Hayman, *Tennessee Williams: Everyone Else is an Audience*, Yale University Press, New York and London, 1985

Donald Spoto, *The Kindness of Strangers: The Life of Tennessee Williams*, Bodley Head, 1985

The playwright's memoirs, not always reliable, but highly readable, include comments on his work as well as his life:
Tennessee Williams, *Memoirs*, W. H. Allen & Co. Ltd, London, 1976

Williams' mother also produced her own memoirs of her son, which are ghost written by Lucy Freeman:
Edwina Dakin Williams, *Remember Me to Tom*, G. P. Putnam's Sons, 1963; Cassell, 1964

Conversations with Tennessee Williams, ed. Albert J. Devlin, University Press of Mississippi, Jackson and London, 1986
    Includes material from a great number of interviews that the playwright granted during his lifetime; covers his life and work

LITERARY CRITICISM

Bloom's Major Dramatists: Tennessee Williams, ed. Harold Bloom, Chelsea House Publishers, 2000
    Critical views on *The Glass Menagerie* can be found on pp. 48–69. Includes Ruby Cohn on 'Sublimating Animal Drives into Esthetics' and Arthur Ganz on 'The Influence of D. H. Lawrence'

Roger Boxill, *Tennessee Williams,* Macmillan Modern Dramatists, London, 1987
    A study of *The Glass Menagerie* can be found on pp. 61–75. Good on staging and symbolism

Twentieth Century Interpretations of *The Glass Menagerie,* ed. R. B. Parker, Prentice Hall, Inc., New Jersey, 1983
    Comprehensive and accessible collection of critical essays. Good coverage of past productions of the play, Williams' influences and dramaturgy

The Cambridge Companion to Tennessee Williams, ed. Matthew C. Roudane, Cambridge University Press, 1997
    An excellent book, which includes a chapter on the play by C. W. E. Bigsby, 'Entering The Glass Menagerie', pp. 29–44. Arthur Miller's comments, quoted in Critical History, can be found on p. 31, as well as comments by early reviewers. Other chapters worth looking at are mentioned separately below

David Savran, *Communists, Cowboys and Queers: The Politics of Masculinity in the Work of Arthur Miller and Tennessee Williams,* University of Minnesota Press, Minneapolis, London, 1992
    Savran makes a number of insightful comments about *The Glass Menagerie*, as well as Williams' other plays. Particularly interesting on gender and dramatic technique

Lester A. Beaurline, '*The Glass Menagerie*: From Story to Play', *Twentieth Century Interpretations of The Glass Menagerie,* op. cit. pp. 44–52

John H. Clum, 'The sacrificial stud and the fugitive female in *Suddenly*

Y

Last Summer, Orpheus Descending, and *Sweet Bird of Youth*', in *The Cambridge Companion to Tennessee Williams*, op. cit. pp. 128–46

Gilbert Debusscher, 'Creative rewriting: European and American influences on the dramas of Tennessee Williams', *The Cambridge Companion to Tennessee Williams*, op. cit. pp. 167–88

Eric Levy, '"Through Soundproof Glass": The Prison of Self-Consciousness in *The Glass Menagerie*', Modern Drama 36, no.4 (December 1993), pp. 529–31

Nancy M. Tischler, 'Romantic textures in Tennessee Williams' plays and short stories', *The Cambridge Companion to Tennessee Williams*, op. cit, pp. 147–66

World Events	**1939**	Arts	Tennessee Williams
Outbreak of Second World War in Europe		Film version of Margaret Mitchell's *Gone With the Wind*, starring Clark Gable and Vivien Leigh Film *The Wizard of Oz*, starring Judy Garland Publication of the novel *The Grapes of Wrath* by John Steinbeck	*American Blues*, a collection of three short plays by Tennessee Williams wins a prize at the Group Theatre Play Contest

World Events	**1940**	Arts	Tennessee Williams
Battle of Britain		*The Long Mirror* by J.B. Priestley is staged Charlie Chaplin directs and stars in the film *The Great Dictator* Publication of the novel *For Whom the Bell Tolls* by Ernest Hemingway	The play *Battle of Angels* is not a success

World Events	**1941**	Arts	Tennessee Williams
USA joins the Allies against the Axis powers in the Second World War		Orson Welles directs and stars in the film *Citizen Kane* Noel Coward's play *Blithe Spirit* is staged The play *Long Day's Journey into Night* by Eugene O'Neill is staged	

World Events	**1942**	Arts	Tennessee Williams
US naval-air victory at Midway Island ends Japanese expansion in the Pacific		Edward Hopper paints *Nighthawks* Publication of the novel *L'Etranger* by Albert Camus	

1943

World Events	Arts	Tennessee Williams
British and American troops land at Salerno	The Rodgers and Hammerstein musical *Oklahoma* is staged Jean-Paul Sartre's essay *Being and Nothingness* is published	Obtains a contract as a scriptwriter for MGM

1944

World Events	Arts	Tennessee Williams
D-Day Allied landings in Normandy	Laurence Olivier directs and stars in the film *Henry V* Bartok's Violin Concerto Jean-Paul Sartre's play *Huis Clos* is staged	*The Glass Menagerie* is staged

1945

World Events	Arts	Tennessee Williams
US President Franklin D. Roosevelt dies. He is succeeded by Harry S. Truman American aircraft drops atomic bombs on Hiroshima and Nagasaki End of Second World War	The play *An Inspector Calls* by J.B. Priestley is staged George Orwell's novel *Animal Farm* is published	Starts work on the play *A Streetcar Named Desire*

World Events	**1946**	Arts	Tennessee Williams
An upsurge of labour unrest cripples large sections of US industry		The play *The Iceman Cometh* by Eugene O'Neill is staged Publication of *A History of Western Philosophy* by Bertrand Russell Publication of the poetry collection *North and South* by Elizabeth Bishop	
	1947		
India and Pakistan become independent		Arthur Miller's play *All My Sons* is staged *The Linden Tree* by J.B. Priestley is staged Henri Cartier-Bresson holds one-man show at New York's Museum of Modern Art	
	1948		
Britain, USA and France cooperate in establishing an airlift to West Berlin Gandhi assassinated in Delhi		British première of *The Glass Menagerie* directed by John Gielgud The play *The Browning Version* by Terence Rattigan is staged Laurence Olivier directs and stars in the film *Hamlet* The novel *La Peste* by Albert Camus is published	

World Events	**1949**	Arts	Tennessee Williams
Chinese Communist People's Republic is proclaimed		The essay *The Second Sex* by Simone de Beauvoir is published Film *The Third Man* by Orson Welles is screened Arthur Miller's play *Death of a Salesman* is staged	British première of *A Streetcar Named Desire* at the Aldwych Theatre, London, directed by Laurence Olivier
	1950		
General MacArthur, commanding the UN forces, launches a counter-offensive against the North Korean invaders in the Korean War		Commercial colour television broadcasting begins in the USA Robert Doisneau produces the photograph *The Kiss for Life* magazine	*The Glass Menagerie* is filmed, directed by Irving Rapper Publication of *The Roman Spring of Mrs Stone*, a novella
	1951		
USA explode the first hydrogen bomb		The film *The African Queen*, starring Humphrey Bogart and Katherine Hepburn, is screened The novel *The Catcher in the Rye* by J.D. Salinger is published	*A Streetcar Named Desire* is filmed, directed by Elia Kazan *The Rose Tattoo* is staged

closure the impression of completeness and finality achieved by the ending of a work of literature

epilogue concluding speech or passage in a work of literature, often summing up or commenting on what has gone before. The epilogue may help to achieve closure

Expressionism A short-lived European artistic movement which started around 1900 in Germany. Expressionism was a revolt against Realism. Instead of attempting to represent the world conventionally and objectively, Expressionist writers and painters show reality distorted by an emotional state of mind

figurative language any form of language that deviates from the plainest expression of meaning is a designated 'a figure of speech'

genre the term for a kind or type of literature

imagery, image in its narrowest sense an image is a word-picture, a description of some visible scene or object. More commonly, imagery refers to the figurative language in a piece of literature (metaphors and similes); or all the words which refer to objects which appeal to the senses and feelings. Thematic imagery is imagery which recurs throughout a work of art

irony saying one thing while you mean another. However, not all ironical statements are easily understood, and characters may not always be aware that they are speaking ironically (this is unconscious irony). Ironic literature characteristically presents a variety of possible points of view about its subject matter. Sometimes the writer will have to rely on the audience sharing values and knowledge in order for his or her meaning to be understood

melodrama any kind of writing which relies on sensational happenings, violent action and improbable events. Characterisation might be simple and flat, rather than complex. Melodrama often relies on stock situations and stereotypes

metaphor a figure of speech in which a word or phrase is applied to an object which it does not literally denote: one thing is described as being another, thus 'carrying over' its associations

modernist writing of the twentieth century which differed from the literary conventions inherited from the nineteenth century

motif some aspect of literature (a type of character, theme or image) which recurs frequently

Naturalism Naturalism was a coherent literary movement of the late nineteenth century, concerned to illustrate a particular kind of realism based on a view of man as inextricably and tragically dominated by the forces of nature within him. In the theatre, naturalistic stage presentation would include realistic ('natural') rather than attention-grabbing acting and lighting styles, and sets would be designed to look like real rooms. When the curtain goes up, the audience is given the impression that they are observing the action through an invisible fourth wall

parody an imitation of a work or style devised so as to ridicule its characteristics

prologue the introductory section to a literary or dramatic work of art

Realism the attempt to portray events and characters realistically in a work of art. Realist authors often concentrate on observing and writing about ordinary people

soliloquy a convention which allows a character to speak directly to the audience

subplot a subsidiary action running parallel with the main plot

symbol a thing that represents or stands for something else by analogy or association

tableau vivant a living picture, a silent and motionless group of actors arranged so as to represent a dramatic scene or event

Rebecca Warren teaches English. She is the author of York Notes Advanced on *King Lear, Othello, The Taming of the Shrew, Richard III, The Mayor of Casterbridge* and *Sylvia Plath's Selected Poems.*

Y

NOTES

York Notes Advanced

Margaret Atwood
Cat's Eye

Margaret Atwood
The Handmaid's Tale

Jane Austen
Emma

Jane Austen
Mansfield Park

Jane Austen
Persuasion

Jane Austen
Pride and Prejudice

Jane Austen
Sense and Sensibility

Alan Bennett
Talking Heads

William Blake
Songs of Innocence and of Experience

Charlotte Brontë
Jane Eyre

Charlotte Brontë
Villette

Emily Brontë
Wuthering Heights

Angela Carter
Nights at the Circus

Geoffrey Chaucer
The Franklin's Prologue and Tale

Geoffrey Chaucer
The Miller's Prologue and Tale

Geoffrey Chaucer
Prologue to the Canterbury Tales

Geoffrey Chaucer
The Wife of Bath's Prologue and Tale

Samuel Taylor Coleridge
Selected Poems

Joseph Conrad
Heart of Darkness

Daniel Defoe
Moll Flanders

Charles Dickens
Bleak House

Charles Dickens
Great Expectations

Charles Dickens
Hard Times

Emily Dickinson
Selected Poems

John Donne
Selected Poems

Carol Ann Duffy
Selected Poems

George Eliot
Middlemarch

George Eliot
The Mill on the Floss

T.S. Eliot
Selected Poems

T.S. Eliot
The Waste Land

F. Scott Fitzgerald
The Great Gatsby

E.M. Forster
A Passage to India

Brian Friel
Translations

Thomas Hardy
Jude the Obscure

Thomas Hardy
The Mayor of Casterbridge

Thomas Hardy
The Return of the Native

Thomas Hardy
Selected Poems

Thomas Hardy
Tess of the d'Urbervilles

Seamus Heaney
Selected Poems from Opened Ground

Nathaniel Hawthorne
The Scarlet Letter

Homer
The Iliad

Homer
The Odyssey

Aldous Huxley
Brave New World

Kazuo Ishiguro
The Remains of the Day

Ben Jonson
The Alchemist

James Joyce
Dubliners

John Keats
Selected Poems

Christopher Marlowe
Doctor Faustus

Christopher Marlowe
Edward II

Arthur Miller
Death of a Salesman

John Milton
Paradise Lost Books I & II

Toni Morrison
Beloved

George Orwell
Nineteen-Eighty-Four

Sylvia Plath
Selected Poems

Alexander Pope
Rape of the Lock and other poems

William Shakespeare
Antony and Cleopatra

William Shakespeare
As You Like It

William Shakespeare
Hamlet

William Shakespeare
King Lear

William Shakespeare
Macbeth

William Shakespeare
Measure for Measure

William Shakespeare
The Merchant of Venice

William Shakespeare
A Midsummer Night's Dream

William Shakespeare
Much Ado About Nothing

William Shakespeare
Othello

William Shakespeare
Richard II

William Shakespeare
Richard III

William Shakespeare
Romeo and Juliet

William Shakespeare
The Taming of the Shrew

ADVANCED LEVEL TITLES (CONTINUED)

William Shakespeare
The Tempest

William Shakespeare
Twelfth Night

William Shakespeare
The Winter's Tale

George Bernard Shaw
Saint Joan

Mary Shelley
Frankenstein

Jonathan Swift
*Gulliver's Travels and A Modest
Proposal*

Alfred, Lord Tennyson
Selected Poems

Virgil
The Aeneid

Alice Walker
The Color Purple

Oscar Wilde
*The Importance of Being
Earnest*

Tennessee Williams
A Streetcar Named Desire

Jeanette Winterson
Oranges Are Not the Only Fruit

John Webster
The Duchess of Malfi

Virginia Woolf
To the Lighthouse

W.B. Yeats
Selected Poems

Metaphysical Poets

GCSE and equivalent levels

Maya Angelou
I Know Why the Caged Bird Sings

Jane Austen
Pride and Prejudice

Alan Ayckbourn
Absent Friends

Elizabeth Barrett Browning
Selected Poems

Robert Bolt
A Man for All Seasons

Harold Brighouse
Hobson's Choice

Charlotte Brontë
Jane Eyre

Emily Brontë
Wuthering Heights

Shelagh Delaney
A Taste of Honey

Charles Dickens
David Copperfield

Charles Dickens
Great Expectations

Charles Dickens
Hard Times

Charles Dickens
Oliver Twist

Roddy Doyle
Paddy Clarke Ha Ha Ha

George Eliot
Silas Marner

George Eliot
The Mill on the Floss

Anne Frank
The Diary of Anne Frank

William Golding
Lord of the Flies

Oliver Goldsmith
She Stoops to Conquer

Willis Hall
The Long and the Short and the Tall

Thomas Hardy
Far from the Madding Crowd

Thomas Hardy
The Mayor of Casterbridge

Thomas Hardy
Tess of the d'Urbervilles

Thomas Hardy
The Withered Arm and other Wessex Tales

L.P. Hartley
The Go-Between

Seamus Heaney
Selected Poems

Susan Hill
I'm the King of the Castle

Barry Hines
A Kestrel for a Knave

Louise Lawrence
Children of the Dust

Harper Lee
To Kill a Mockingbird

Laurie Lee
Cider with Rosie

Arthur Miller
The Crucible

Arthur Miller
A View from the Bridge

Robert O'Brien
Z for Zachariah

Frank O'Connor
My Oedipus Complex and Other Stories

George Orwell
Animal Farm

J.B. Priestley
An Inspector Calls

J.B. Priestley
When We Are Married

Willy Russell
Educating Rita

Willy Russell
Our Day Out

J.D. Salinger
The Catcher in the Rye

William Shakespeare
Henry IV Part 1

William Shakespeare
Henry V

William Shakespeare
Julius Caesar

William Shakespeare
Macbeth

William Shakespeare
The Merchant of Venice

William Shakespeare
A Midsummer Night's Dream

William Shakespeare
Much Ado About Nothing

William Shakespeare
Romeo and Juliet

William Shakespeare
The Tempest

William Shakespeare
Twelfth Night

George Bernard Shaw
Pygmalion

Mary Shelley
Frankenstein

R.C. Sherriff
Journey's End

Rukshana Smith
Salt on the Snow

John Steinbeck
Of Mice and Men

Robert Louis Stevenson
Dr Jekyll and Mr Hyde

Jonathan Swift
Gulliver's Travels

Robert Swindells
Daz 4 Zoe

Mildred D. Taylor
Roll of Thunder, Hear My Cry

Mark Twain
Huckleberry Finn

James Watson
Talking in Whispers

Edith Wharton
Ethan Frome

William Wordsworth
Selected Poems

A Choice of Poets

Mystery Stories of the Nineteenth Century including The Signalman

Nineteenth Century Short Stories

Poetry of the First World War

Six Women Poets